M000227169

"Prayer is the key to responding t Word. Prayer is the power to love, ᴛʜᴇ ᴘᴏᴡᴇʀ ᴛᴏ ᴏʙᴇy, ᴛʜᴇ power to walk out our faith and calling. For us, prayer has been the super glue to keep us happily married and in ministry for almost four decades. And with everything in life, when you want to learn or improve or hone a skill, you go to the Master, the One who is the best. And Jesus is that Chief Expert. Janet McHenry, in *The Complete Guide to the Prayers of Jesus*, has made the prayers of Christ come alive, and she has also laid the path for all of us to pray, and see answers to prayer, by learning a Christlike model that can draw each of us closer to the heart of our Creator, Abba Father."

—Pastor Bill Farrel and Pam Farrel, co-directors of Love-Wise,
authors of forty-five books including *Men Are Like Waffles—Women
Are Like Spaghetti, The 10 Best Decisions a Couple Can Make,*
and *A Couple's Journey with God*

"*The Complete Guide to the Prayers of Jesus* more than lives up to its name. Not only is it wonderfully complete—relishing the substance of all of the Savior's teaching on prayer—it is also a fantastic guide. Readers will be instructed, inspired, and motivated like never before to follow Jesus in a life of prayer. Great for groups. Highly recommended."

—Bill Giovannetti, senior pastor,
Neighborhood Church, Redding, CA

"As a very busy mom of ten kids, I know I wouldn't survive this life journey without a continual lifestream of prayer. I was delighted, then, to find Janet McHenry's book that shows us how Jesus communicated with his heavenly Father. You will be blessed to find everything about Jesus' prayer life in this book—everything he taught about prayer as well as all of his prayers and prayer practices. Learning more about Jesus' prayer life has helped me lift up my family as we walk out life together."

—Tricia Goyer, bestselling author of more than sixty books,
including *Walk It Out: The Radical Result
of Living God's Word One Step at a Time*

"Every good teacher finds a way to make a subject come to life in the midst of the important details. Janet is a good teacher. She takes us deeper into the meaning and application of the prayers of Jesus. The effect of this book is more than the acquiring of knowledge. You will feel compelled to pray, and as you do, align your heart with the themes and words found in Christ's prayers."

—Robin Jones Gunn, bestselling author of *Praying for Your Future Husband* and *Victim of Grace*

"If you long to pray more effectively, read this book. Based on the prayers of Jesus, Janet reveals the secrets of connecting with God in an intimate, ongoing way. You'll learn how to listen to God's voice, deal with temptation, pray for specific needs, and practice forgiveness. Every Christian needs this book."

—Carol Kent, speaker and author, *He Holds My Hand: Experiencing God's Presence & Protection*

"When I want to become better in any subject, I look for an expert in that area. Janet has written about the value of prayerwalking in her previous books. What I love most about this book is that Janet went to the expert on prayer, Jesus Christ, and studied how he prayed. As we study when and how Jesus prayed we will learn the secrets of powerful praying."

—Carole Lewis, First Place 4 Health director emeritus, author of *Give God a Year, Change Your Life Forever*

"Have you ever echoed the disciple's request, 'Lord, teach us to pray'? Could your own prayer life use some tweaking or, better yet, an infusion of power and purpose? Then join me in welcoming Janet McHenry's new book *The Complete Guide to the Prayers of Jesus: What Jesus Prayed and How It Can Change Your Life Today*. Through a lifetime journey of drawing near to God in prayer, McHenry lifts up more than a dozen different instances in the life of Jesus when he prayed intentionally—in times of praise, crisis, temptation, despair, trouble, and personal struggle, for friends, forgiveness, blessing, and provision. In this abundance of biblical teaching, we discover not only how to pray but also how to apply these scriptural principles to our own lives. This is the beauty of the author's authentic stories of grappling with prayer in the trenches of marriage, parenthood, teaching, and writing—if she can do it, so can we! My favorite parts were her biblically based prayers that so beautifully concluded and summarized each chapter—I will be praying those even after I've finished the book. If you really want to ignite your prayer life, look no further than Jesus himself and let Janet McHenry's wonderful new book be your guide."

—Lucinda Secrest McDowell, author of
Ordinary Graces and *Dwelling Places*

"The author beautifully weaves together examples from her life with those of Jesus in his, reminding us that God hears and answers our prayers, regardless of the situation. This practical and inspirational book will inspire and renew your prayer life."

—Karen O'Connor, author of *When God Answers Your Prayers: Inspiring Stories of How God Comes Through in the Nick of Time*

"Practical, thought-provoking, and worth pondering, Janet Holm McHenry's *The Complete Guide to the Prayers of Jesus* is an important resource for both the prayer newbie and the well-practiced. I've bookmarked the praise chart to refer to often."

—Cynthia Ruchti, author of more than twenty books, including *A Fragile Hope* and *As My Parents Age*

"Let Janet Holm McHenry's *The Complete Guide to the Prayers of Jesus* lead you not only into deeper prayer experiences but into a deeper relationship with Jesus himself."

—Linda Evans Shepherd, author of
When You Don't Know What to Pray

"What a beautiful and intimate look at prayer from the life of Jesus! This book will not only stir and challenge you toward a life of prayer, it will give you tools to cultivate a living, ongoing conversation with the One who loves you more than you could possibly know."

—Joanna Weaver, author of *Having a Mary Heart in a Martha World*

"Janet McHenry has a way of always motivating me to pray. Her latest book, *The Complete Guide to the Prayers of Jesus*, will encourage you to raise your prayer life to a new level in both practical and personal ways as you learn from the Master himself."

—Bill West, Senior Pastor, The Bridge Church, Reno, NV

THE COMPLETE GUIDE
to the
Prayers
of
JESUS

JANET HOLM MCHENRY

BETHANYHOUSE
a division of Baker Publishing Group
Minneapolis, Minnesota

To the Lord Jesus Christ:
I pray these words are worthy
of the calling you have on my life,
but even more so, are worthy
of having your name on the cover
and within these pages.

Contents

Foreword   11

Acknowledgments   13

Introduction: Jesus, Our Mentor in Prayer   15

1. Jesus Listened in Prayer   23

2. Jesus' Prayer in the Face of Temptation   37

3. Jesus' Prayer for Daily Needs 47

4. Jesus' Prayer of Praise   59

5. Jesus' Prayer of Thanksgiving   68

6. Jesus' Prayer in Trouble   78

7. Jesus' Prayer for Himself   86

8. Jesus' Prayer for Friends   97

9. Jesus' Prayer for the Church   108

10. Jesus' Prayer over Critical Decisions   118

11. Jesus' Prayer for Forgiveness   129

Contents

12. Jesus' Prayer in Abandonment   139

13. Jesus' Prayer of Submission   149

14. Jesus' Prayers of Blessing   159

   Conclusion: Jesus Lives to Pray   167

   Notes   171

Foreword

When I want to learn something, I want to learn from the best. One of the best ways of learning or honing a skill is to be mentored by an expert—someone who knows the intricacies and the secrets, and who knows from experience the challenges. In being mentored, I will be afforded more than information and knowledge; I will learn from my mentor's life. My mentor will lead me hands-on through the new skill until it becomes my second nature. My mentor will reproduce his own experience in me.

Janet introduces us to Jesus, Prayer Mentor. The living, indwelling, right-now Jesus will teach us to pray in real time. From him, we will learn more than prayer theology, though we will learn that as well.

Jesus knows what makes prayer work, and he is perfectly willing to teach us the secret. In my own life, I replaced the thought of saying prayers—sandwiching words between "Dear God" and "Amen"—with the awareness of being in the flow of his power and provision. I expanded my definition of prayer so that it includes the continual interaction between the material and the spiritual realm—sometimes articulated, but often simply an inarticulate flow between his heart and mine.

E. Stanley Jones articulates it this way in *Abundant Living*: "Gracious Christ, teach me to pray. For if I fall down here, I fall down everywhere—anemia spreads through my whole being. Give me the mind to pray, the love to pray, the will to pray. Let prayer be the aroma of every act, the atmosphere of every thought, my native air. In Your name. Amen."[1]

Janet shows us that Jesus as our Prayer Mentor will impart to us his own heart and mind, not simply to teach us his methods, but to reproduce his prayer life in us. We see clearly in the gospels that Jesus' life of prayer showed up in his life of power. Janet makes it clear in this comprehensive look at the prayer life of Jesus that this is his goal for us. That prayer will not be just a ritual or a discipline, but instead will be life and breath.

Even for Jesus, keeping his heart connected to the Father's required deliberate intention and decision. Jesus was one in nature with the Father from the beginning, but was a separate being. He chose submission as the very tenor of his life, but he also chose to obey in the moment as the moment arose.

As he walked out his days in step with the Father through prayer, his perfectly choreographed obedience seemed to come effortlessly. He seemed to know instinctively what the Father was doing at any given juncture. Doing the Father's will appeared to be the natural cadence of his life. The connection was kept always fresh through prayer.

Janet has written a book that will pull you into the very same kind of connected relationship with him that he had with his Father as he lived life in the nature of a man. It is well researched, thorough, and engagingly written.

Jennifer Kennedy Dean

Author of *Live a Praying Life* and
executive director of the Praying Life Foundation

Acknowledgments

The writing of this book came during a very challenging season when I was completely dependent upon prayer, encouragement from God's Word, and great portions of grace from my family, especially my husband, Craig; my mom, Doris Holm; my daughters, Rebekah Perez and Bethany Mariconda; my sister and brother-in-law, Roberta and Steve Martinez; my niece, Rachel Stewart; and my sister-in-law, Lisa Puglisi. It took a Holm/McHenry village to write a book and move my mom and her ninety years of love from Wheel C Ranch into her new Holm-sweet-Holm. As Dad used to say, "Wheel C," which I'm realizing truly was a metaphor for expectant prayer.

Writing *The Complete Guide to the Prayers of Jesus* was such a privilege that every time I sat down to study, research, write notes, or put words on the computer screen, I was completely humbled that I could be given this opportunity. Thank you, Kim Bangs, Sharon Hodge, Leeanna Nelson, David Horton, and all the folks at Bethany House. I am so thankful for you all. To God be the glory.

Introduction

Jesus, Our Mentor in Prayer

From his spot at the head of the table, Jesus looked around the dimly lit room. Peter's wife and mother-in-law stood wiping the cooking pot and bowls near the fire. He had grown fond of them, as well as their offering each evening of well-seasoned fish and lentil stew, sopped up with a hearty chunk of bread. For months now his Capernaum hosts nightly had spread mats on the floor around the rough-hewn table in the small main room, for him, Peter, James, John, and a handful of other followers. Though the others were talking quietly—occasionally glancing over at Jesus to ask a question—a tension was building inside of him. He had to meet with his Father.

As Jesus stood and walked toward the door, the others looked up but did not protest his leaving the relative warmth of the small stone home in the dead of winter. They understood. He often withdrew to quiet places to pray.

Jesus stepped out into the darkness, draped his head with his white linen covering, and pulled his woolen upper garment around himself more snugly. The cold evening air smarted on his uncovered hands and sandaled feet. But at least the streets were quiet. When the sun had fallen late that afternoon, the crowds of people seeking a healing touch or even just a word from Jesus had slowly disbursed. They would seek him out the next day . . . and the next . . . and the next. Their needs were never ending, like the lapping waves on the nearby Sea of Galilee.

The water moved in darkness to his left, but this evening's meeting place was in the hills to his right. Jesus headed toward a well-worn path up the mountain's slope with much on his mind and heart. His teachings and miracles were drawing attention. Seekers were listening to his interpretations of the law at synagogues in various towns throughout Galilee, but the Pharisees were beginning to challenge him.

When Jesus forgave the sins of the paralytic man, the Pharisees said he was speaking blasphemy—considered the most serious sin because it was cursing God. When his followers gleaned some grain in local fields after the harvest, the Pharisees accused him of dishonoring the Sabbath, a day set aside solely for worship of the Lord God. Even worse, when he healed a man with a shriveled hand on the Sabbath, they grew furious and began plotting against him.

Clearly, his ministry could come to an end soon—and he needed his Father's guidance. Who would carry the message of life-giving grace when he was gone? More than a hundred people were following him daily as he traveled from town to town. Yet who among them should be his disciples?

One man—a teacher of the law—had even said, "Teacher, I will follow you wherever you go."

Jesus had responded that even though foxes have holes and birds have nests, he had no place to sleep at night. Who would follow him into homelessness?

Another follower had said he would follow Jesus, but asked him to "first let me go and bury my father."

"Follow me," Jesus replied, "and let the dead bury the dead."

Jesus knew that the challenges he was facing paled in view of the Cross ahead. Would any disciple follow him, pray for him, understand his calling and purpose, and remain faithful after his death?

His Father would know.

After a trek of twenty minutes, Jesus reached a mountainside spot away from the sounds of the city. He turned toward Capernaum, its home fires barely visible under the cloud-covered moon. And he prayed.

"Abba, Father . . ."

The damp night air settled over him as the fires gradually dimmed in the city below. Jesus prostrated himself on the rocky hillside.

"Abba, Father . . ."

As the moon faded to nothing behind the clouds, Jesus heard a stirring behind him in the rocks above. *Just a family of hyraxes digging new trails. No one but the watchman is awake at this third watch of the night.*

"Abba, Father . . ."

Then he fell silent, listening for more than the wind or the hillside animals or the lapping waves below. He would stay and listen for his Father's words . . . and he would know which twelve should be his apostles, the message bearers of lifesaving truth.

Eventually night turned to dawn, the sun rising behind the mountains east of the Sea of Galilee as a brilliant golden ball surrounded by an aura of orange that filled the sky and warmed the blues of the sea. Jesus raised his arms toward heaven, thankful to the Father for hearing him and for speaking into his heart, mind, and soul.

A short time later he slipped back down the mountain into Capernaum, stepped through Peter's door, and shared morning bread with the drowsy disciples. And he announced the names of the chosen Twelve—one of whom would eventually betray him, one of whom would deny him, and all of whom would temporarily turn away in just over a year's time.

But peace rested on Jesus' countenance as he looked among the group of ordinary men that included fishermen, a tax collector, a revolutionary, a quibbler, and others. Because he had spent the evening in prayer and would continue to pray through the rest of his days on earth, he could rest in the confidence that his Father was guiding him step by step in his walk to the Cross.

In the early years of my Christian walk, I never really thought about learning to pray by taking a close look at Jesus' prayers and his prayer life in general. Even in my growing-up years in a faithful, churchgoing family, we only prayed grace over dinner and "Now I lay me down to sleep. . . ." In my church we recited beautiful prayers from a book. But we approached everyday life with German/Finnish resolve and faced big decisions with comparison charts, lists, and logic—not prayer.

When I gave my heart to Christ in college, I had an immediate hunger to learn more about the Savior I now loved with all my being—an insatiable desire to read his Word. But somehow I was sidetracked with theological studies about grace, forgiveness, redemption, transformation, and sanctification. And while I read, studied, and even taught the Bible from one end to the other, I lost sight of prayer. So my own growing family prayed grace over dinner and "Now I lay me down to sleep. . . ."

Certainly, prayer darts were thrown toward the skies in frantic moments. For goodness' sake, I had four children who loved to torment each other, it seemed, thus tormenting my husband, Craig, and me.

Lord, please stop that child from being such a tease.

Father, do they really need to climb out of their windows at night?

A cigarette in the wash, Lord? Why is that child smoking?

Yes, I had read the book that taught prayer is conversation with God. And yes, I'm a pretty good conversationalist. Yes, I know questioning and listening are integral parts of prayer. Yes, I know that conversation is not all about me.

> *How was your day, God?*
> *Not so good?*
> *Neither was mine. Here's the deal. . . .*

You see, for me, prayer was still something on my to-do list. Bible reading, check. Prayer, check. Shower, check.

It still hadn't quite clicked that prayer is like breathing. You need it for a vital faithwalk. Blow the bad stuff out, breathe in the good.

And then I began prayerwalking.

After our second child headed off to college, I decided to work on my health. And because I'm a good multitasker, I decided to check Prayer off the daily list, too, and pray as I walked. One morning a few months into the routine, I saw what I call a Single Daddy's Ballet. In the dark hours of the morning, the young man handed over his blanketed toddler girl to the day-care worker at the center's entrance, and that blanketed bundle said, "Bye, Daddy, love you." Because of that ten-second vignette, God led me to switch my prayer focus from self to sight—and still, as I walk or drive or stand in a checkout line, I pray for whatever God puts in my eyesight.

This new focus made me determined to learn as much as I could about prayer, so I began searching for evidence of it in the

Bible, marking the margins all the way from Genesis to Revelation with a circled *P* whenever I found a reference (hundreds and hundreds of them)—someone praying, God speaking to his people, instruction about prayer.

I also have spent a chunk of life studying Jesus' prayer life: what he taught about prayer, what he did as a practice, and his prayers themselves. It's interesting that John starts his biography of the Christ with, "In the beginning was the Word, and the Word was with God, and the Word was God. He was with God in the beginning" (John 1:1–2). But millennia after that beginning of life on earth, the Word then became the emissary on earth. The Word came to us, leaving his heavenly home with the Father to provide a way for us to establish an eternal connection and conversation with the Father.

Separation from the Father must have been hard. Those of you who have experienced sending a child off to college, or off on a plane, or even off with Grandma and Grandpa for a vacation understand that dichotomy of emotions. Your beloved child is headed for a grand adventure—one that will bring much good. But the separation is painful. A part of your very being has been ripped away, it seems. The one compensation—especially in these modern times—is that you can communicate fairly easily with phone calls, texts, messages, and more.

So, too, did Jesus the Son, the Word made flesh, communicate with God the Father—through prayer. Old-school FaceTime. The Son of Man instantly in the presence of the Creator.

This wasn't so new. Jesus was born into a family that prayed. His mother Mary sang a song of praise when she found out she was pregnant (Luke 1:46–55). The Lord sent angels to reassure Mary's fiancé, Joseph, that the Holy Spirit had conceived the child. The Lord also nudged Joseph to go into exile when King Herod went on a killing spree of baby boys in hopes of eliminating the Messiah. Family members Elizabeth and Zechariah praised God for his goodness in bringing them a child in their old age. Jesus' family naturally went to the Father with praise and for direction.

Jesus would grow "in wisdom and in stature and in favor with God and all the people" (Luke 2:52 NLT) because his short walk on earth would be done prayerfully. He had daily rhythms of prayer, times when he got alone with God. He lived intentionally with guidance from the Lord God. In anticipation of challenge and suffering, he looked up for strength.

As we also learn to grow in wisdom, stature, and favor with God, we can look to our Master Teacher and his prayers—not necessarily to copy or memorize—but to inform and develop our own conversations with the Father. Each of the fourteen chapters in this book examines the significance of one of Jesus' prayers, incorporating his related teachings and personal practices. From them we can gather insights about how to make prayer more natural in our lives—a first response rather than a last resort. You'll also find at the end of each chapter a prayer for you that I hope will help you pray intentionally and strategically, as each is based on God's Word. I have also included questions for study and reflection as you are growing in prayer.

I am excited for you to discover more about Jesus' prayer life, because I believe it will teach you how to develop a deeper relationship with our Father in heaven. No matter what your faith background, you can look to Jesus as your personal mentor, teacher, and example. From him we learn that prayer is as essential as breathing. Breathe in his words and teachings, reader, and you will find that your new life of prayer fills you with the strength and direction you'll need for anything that blows your way.

Chapter 1

Jesus Listened in Prayer

I was having the hardest time getting my high school seniors to pay attention in English class as I prepped them for their senior play performance. The biggest distractor was a beautiful, blue-eyed, long-haired brunette with an engaging smile and chatty manner. She sat in the middle of the classroom and seemingly loved to comment on my every remark.

Finally, I stopped what I was saying and looked pointedly at her. The rest of the room got the hint, but she kept chatting with her neighbors. Even Robert, the one who competed with her for the Most Talkative Award, had stopped and then blurted out, "Rebekah, stop talking! Your mom's trying to say something."

Yes, she was my daughter—our oldest and the most outgoing of our four children. She was the first to fall victim to having her mother as the English teacher for all juniors and seniors in our small high school, and she probably compensated for her embarrassment of me by chatting it up—a lot.

Many of us fail to listen, don't we? In conversations, we often are silently preparing for our next brilliant comment instead of truly absorbing what a friend is trying to communicate. As we jockey for the most witty remark or make our mental list of how to solve our friends' many problems, we might miss the verbal nudges that would move us the most or the emotional nuances that could give us insight to meet our friends' otherwise veiled needs.

There are three recorded instances of Jesus' hearing from his heavenly Father. It's interesting that the first recorded instance of his prayer life in the gospels is also one that results in audibly hearing from the Father.

Jesus, just starting his ministry, arrived at the Judean area of the Jordan River, roughly sixty miles south of his hometown of Nazareth. His second cousin, John, was preaching and baptizing at the river. John had traveled from the hill country of Judea, undoubtedly near Jerusalem, because his father, Zechariah, served in the temple there as a priest. (For geography aficionados: Nazareth is in the region of Galilee, which lies to the west of the Sea of Galilee in the north. Judea is the area south of Samaria, which lies between Galilee and Judea. The Jordan River runs from the north into and then out of the Sea of Galilee, then ends at the Dead Sea to the south. Within Judea were Jerusalem, Bethlehem to the south, and Bethany to the east.)

At the start of his ministry, Jesus approached John to be baptized in the Jordan River. At first John objected: "I need to be baptized by you, and do you come to me?" (Matthew 3:14). However, Jesus replied, "Let it be so now; it is proper for us to do this to fulfill all righteousness" (v. 15). With that, John consented, and the moment after Jesus rose from the water, heaven opened, and the Spirit of God descended on Jesus. Gospel writers Matthew, Mark, and Luke reported that the Spirit alighted on Christ like a dove (Matthew 3:16; Mark 1:10; Luke 3:22). God was in this place—not only in the person of Jesus Christ but also through the voice of his Father—because they all heard a voice from heaven: "This is my Son, whom I love; with him I am well pleased" (Matthew 3:17).

Mark and Luke reported this incident almost exactly as Matthew did. However, instead of *"This* is my Son," they wrote, *"You* are my Son" (Mark 1:11; Luke 3:22, emphasis added). No matter whether the word was *this* or *you,* clearly the Father was affirming Jesus in three ways: first, that Jesus was God's son; second, that he loved Jesus; and lastly, that he was pleased with Jesus' decision to submit to baptism. Jesus modeled baptism for all who would believe in him—an act of obedience that would represent a change of heart, "a sorrow for sin and a determination to lead a holy life."[1] What we can learn from this first instance of the Father's audibly spoken words is that one purpose of listening prayer can be to affirm a believer.

Listen Up

Another possible purpose for God's speaking directly to us could be to get us to pay attention. After Jesus had taught and healed . . . and taught and healed, he began trying to explain to his disciples that the Jewish elders, chief priests, and teachers of the law were going to persecute him. Also, while he would be killed at their hand, he would resurrect from the dead on the third day (Matthew 16:21). However, little of this sunk in, apparently. In fact, Peter said, "Never, Lord! This shall never happen to you!" (v. 22). They still did not understand completely who Jesus was and his purpose on earth.

So Jesus taught some more, and then about a week later took Peter, James, and John up a high mountain to pray, and his appearance changed (Luke 9:28–29). Scripture uses the term *transfigured*, which in that context meant his "face shone like the sun, and his clothes became as white as the light" (Matthew 17:2), as bright "as a flash of lightning" (Luke 9:29). And then two important figures of the Old Testament, Moses and Elijah, appeared and began talking with Jesus.

While all of this was transpiring, the disciples were a bit drowsy. Perhaps the climb up the mountain had fatigued them. Once fully awake, however, they saw their transfigured Messiah saying good-bye to the heaven-bound Moses and Elijah. Then the disciples were impressed! In fact, they were so impressed that Peter spoke without thinking—again: "Master, it is good for us to be here. Let us put up three shelters—one for you, one for Moses and one for Elijah" (Luke 9:33). Scripture tells us that he did not know what he was saying—but we probably could have assumed that. Peter often spoke without forethought.

Then came the Rebekah-stop-talking moment. Even while Peter's mouth was still in motion, a bright cloud surrounded them and a voice from the cloud said, "This is my Son, whom I love; with him I am well pleased. Listen to him!" (Matthew 17:5). A slightly different version, "This is my Son, *whom I have chosen*; listen to him," is recorded in Luke 9:35 (emphasis added). Though Christ had taught them that he was going to suffer, die, and resurrect from the dead, they were in denial. Though he had taken them up the mountain to reinforce this message, and though his body was transfigured into light, his key disciples still did not understand the seriousness of what lay ahead. Even if they had believed Jesus was the Messiah, the Son of the living God, they did not understand what the Messiah must do to bring salvation to man. It hadn't even sunk in that Christ was the fulfillment of the law given to Moses and the fulfillment of the words of the prophets such as Elijah.

Peter wanted to set up tabernacle-type tents—one each for Moses, Elijah, and Jesus, as though Jesus were just another bearer of good news, not the finality of it. Peter may have thought he was acting as a wonderful host—providing shelter for the revered visitors. Peter, James, and John may also have been excited to think they would be part of the history of God's work on earth—the recipients of others' praise in generations to come, such as they themselves had given Moses and Elijah. Things had not been going well. After all, by this point Jesus was the target of the Pharisees and other Jewish officials, who felt threatened by his growing following. Now, with the presence and seeming approval of Moses and Elijah, perhaps Peter, James, and John were seeing the potential of being in the cool group on campus, as opposed to the victims of the school bullies.

So it is at this very moment that the Father interrupted the wayward-thinking disciples. A bright cloud suddenly appeared, then enveloped them. This was no ordinary mist, as its presence frightened them when they entered it. The Greek *nephelē* for this word *cloud* gives some insight as to why the disciples were alarmed. This is a definitely shaped cloud, not a spattering of white wisps such as you might see from the window of an ascending airplane. This transfiguration cloud had a form to it, like the one that covered Israel when the Hebrews were crossing the Red Sea or those of John's apocalyptic visions in Revelation.[2] If the transfiguration cloud were like the ones of Exodus times, there may have been accompanying thunder and lightning, as well as a trumpet blast. It could have been pillar-shaped, such as the protective, old-school GPS cloud that led the Israelites from Egypt.

But then seemingly that cloud *spoke*—imagine how that would amp up your anxiety—with the Father's voice coming from it. *Listen to him,* the Father said. *This is my Son; listen to him. I love him; listen to him. I am pleased with what he is doing; listen to him.* In other words, *Stop talking . . . pay attention.* Just as a teacher might ask a student, "Did you just hear what I said?" the Father needed to interrupt the disciples' off-track thinking to point them in the right direction. Their focus needed to be on Jesus.

After this dramatic scene, the disciples seemed to process better. They saw that Moses and Elijah had vanished, and

Jesus told them not to tell anyone what they had seen until the "Son of Man had risen from the dead" (Mark 9:9). They did keep the incident to themselves but discussed what he might have meant by "rising from the dead" (v. 10). Seemingly assessing the bigger picture, they asked Jesus why the teachers of the law were teaching that Elijah had to come first. Jesus responded,

> "To be sure, Elijah does come first, and restores all things. Why then is it written that the Son of Man must suffer much and be rejected? But I tell you, Elijah has come, and they have done to him everything they wished, just as it is written about him."
>
> Mark 9:12–13

The Father had said, "Listen to him," and Jesus' response to their question provided more evidence that Jesus was, in fact, the Messiah, since John the Baptist was the prophet-in-the-wild/Elijah figure who effectively provided the forum for the Spirit's anointing of Jesus after the physical act of baptism.

So this second example of listening prayer is again in a public forum, affirming Christ as the Son, but also clearly indicating to Peter, James, and John that they needed to listen to him. Similarly, God's words to us today may be a listen-up message. We may be completely off track about a direction we are taking in our lives—such as with a job search or a relationship—and may need a voice-in-a-cloud pillar to shake us up, wake us up, and make us see the Truth that may be on the other side of our self-focused blinders.

The third example of Jesus' hearing from his heavenly Father occurred closer to the Cross. It was the week of Passover. Great crowds of people who had come into Jerusalem for the Passover Feast had heard that Jesus also was on his way there. As he approached, the people ran out to meet him and laid palm branches for his tired, traveled feet to tread upon.

"Hosanna!" they cried. "Blessed is he who comes in the name of the Lord!" (John 12:13).

Actually, they were quoting a psalm: "O Lord, save us; O Lord, grant us success" (Psalm 118:25). *Hosanna* was a Hebrew cry for help: "Save, we pray."[3] They were happy to see this Jesus, who made the blind to see and the lame to walk. Maybe he would fix their problems, too.

John recorded the addition of "Blessed is the King of Israel!" Everyone wanted to meet the miracle man, the one called king of the Jews. Some had heard about his raising Lazarus from the dead, just two miles east in Bethany. The crowds around Jesus annoyed the religious Pharisees to no end, the gist of their collective conversation being, "See, this is getting us nowhere. Look how the whole world has gone after him!" The crowd wasn't calling *them* Lord. The crowd wasn't gathering around *them* looking for a healer and teacher. The crowd wasn't laying palm branches for *their* tired feet.

As a group of Greek worshipers came into Jerusalem, they, too, wanted to see Jesus. The attention and pressure certainly bore heavily upon him, and Jesus responded:

> "The hour has come for the Son of Man to be glorified. I tell you the truth, unless a kernel of wheat falls to the ground and dies, it remains only a single seed. But if it dies, it produces many seeds. The man who loves his life will lose it, while the man who hates his life in this world will keep it for eternal life. Whoever serves me must follow me; and where I am, my servant also will be. My Father will honor the one who serves me."
>
> John 12:23–26

Say what? The disciples, the piqued Greeks, and the Feast crowds were probably all there, looking for the next miracle and listening for some clue as to who Jesus really was. They may have been expecting him to say, "Yes, I am the next and final king of Israel. I am the prophesied Messiah. I am." But instead, he spoke of seed and servanthood. Uncertainty and even confusion settled over the people, as Jesus continued,

> "Now my heart is troubled, and what shall I say? 'Father, save me from this hour'? No, it was for this very reason I came to this hour. Father, glorify your name!"
>
> John 12:27–28

Jesus knew his time had come to provide a way for salvation to all who would believe in him. His purpose on earth was to point people to his heavenly Father. Thus, he prayed that the Father's name be glorified.

For the third time we have a recorded response from the heavenly Father: "I have glorified it, and will glorify it again" (v. 28). And we don't need to guess at the reason for these audible words from God, as Jesus explained this to the crowd, some of whom reported that the voice from heaven—no cloud this time—sounded like thunder or the voice of an angel. We all know what thunder sounds like—but the voice of an angel? In any case, we have an interpreter:

> Jesus said, "This voice was for your benefit, not mine. Now is the time for judgment on this world; now the prince of this world will be driven out. But I, when I am lifted up from the earth, will draw all men to myself."
>
> John 12:30–32

The Father's words were not for his Son's "sake" (NASB), to bolster or affirm or encourage Jesus; they were to benefit those within hearing—to convince them that Jesus had the authority to call God his Father, that he indeed was God's Son.

And how exactly did those sparse words benefit the disciples, Greeks, and crowd in general? When the Father thundered from

heaven with his words and when Jesus said those words were for them not him, the people took note. The crowd had been listening and had questions—important ones that could lead to faith and following. In response to Jesus' statement "when I am lifted up," they wanted to know how or why Jesus would say the Son of Man, the Christ—*ho Christos* in the Greek, "the anointed one"—would be lifted up, since they'd been taught he (the Messiah) would remain forever. There was an immediate follow-up question: "Who is this 'Son of Man'?" (John 12:34). The puzzle of hundreds of years could be solved right then and there during that Passover Feast week. What a celebration that would be, indeed, if the carpenter from Nazareth, who was claiming he was the Son of Man, the Christ, the Messiah, proved to be the One for whom they had been waiting.

For those who can read through a metaphor, Jesus provided the answer.

> "You are going to have the light just a little while longer. Walk while you have the light, before darkness overtakes you. The man who walks in the dark does not know where he is going. Put your trust in the light while you have it, so that you may become sons of light."

> John 12:35–36

People wait for signs of spiritual truth, but when they see them, they still don't believe. Hundreds of miracles were performed (the town of Capernaum, for example, was denounced by Jesus for not repenting after the miracles worked there, Matthew 11:23 tells us), and yet people called for more. Jesus spoke at their level with stories pointing toward truth about eternity, but still there were questions. Even a voice of heaven for their benefit that would shake them to their very core was not enough.

31

Hearing from God

So what are we to do with this listening prayer? How do we get God's feedback? Will he answer us? And if he did, would that be with an audible voice? Perhaps. In an old evangelical standard, *Prayer: Conversing with God*, author Rosalind Rinker contends, "Prayer is a dialogue between two persons who love each other."[4] However, some would argue that the Bible does not teach that prayer is conversation. One scholar writes, "If we approach prayer as a verbal dialogue, we'll no doubt be disappointed."[5] Perhaps. However, we do see examples of conversation between God and man in the Bible. Adam, Cain, Noah, and Hagar talked *with* God—not just *at* him. Abraham negotiated for the city of Sodom in Genesis 18. Scripture records many conversations with Moses, including God's call to Moses to lead the Israelites out of Egypt (Exodus 3–4).

And on the road to Damascus, Christian-hater Saul had a conversation with Jesus that led him to faith and changed his life. Some say that was then, but this is now. Perhaps—but if personal experience is evidence that God doesn't speak, personal experience should also be valid to affirm that he does. While I've not heard audibly from God often, there have been at least two times in my life when he has spoken clearly to me. The words were so real to me that they could have been audible, but probably were just implanted within me.

The first time, I was attending a women's retreat in the California Sierra Nevada at a church camp under the monstrous Ponderosa pines. As one session was ending, the speaker encouraged us to "find a rock, sit on it, and wait until God speaks." While I was a bit skeptical, I found a rock and prayed something like, *Okay, God, I'm ready. Fire away.* I honestly think it was just a matter of minutes before I heard, *I want you to write for me.* Because that was such a surprise and because I really did not know what it meant, I paid attention. What would it mean to write for God? Yes, I had a journalism degree, but I was not writing at the time and knew little of the Christian publishing industry. Within a year's time, however, I had attended three week-long Christian writers conferences and was beginning to sell articles to Christian magazines.

The other time I remember hearing God's voice, I was driving our four kids to my parents' house for the weekend. The whole three hours they were going nuts, teasing each other and continually asking me to stop for this and that. Two miles from my parents' home the youngest, Bethany, a toddler, kept saying, "Cows! Cows!" She had remembered there were dairy cows just beyond the upcoming intersection along the road in rural Sacramento. Though I said, "No, another day," the other three begged me to stop. "Just for a second, Mom. What would it hurt?" There was another voice I heard, too: *Stop.* None of the kids had said it, but it left such a strong impression, I quickly moved my foot from the accelerator to the brake as I approached the intersection. In the next instant, a car raced through the intersection from my right to the left. The other car had run the stop sign, and had I continued without braking, our car would have been T-boned with the probability of serious injury or even death for at least some of us.

While I am confident there have been other times God has spoken to me—somehow within my spirit—these are the only two instances I remember, the one different from the other. The first changed my career path significantly, and the second saved my children's lives. For the first I was quietly waiting to hear from him; the second time occurred in the midst of my children's chatter. Both were pay-attention situations. *Pay attention, Janet: Write for me. Go! Pay attention: Stop!* Had I shaken off either of those directions from the Lord, my life would be significantly different today.

How do we listen to God in prayer? Mother Teresa wrote,

In the silence of the heart God speaks. If you face God in prayer
and silence, God will speak to you. Then you will know that
you are nothing. It is only when you realize your nothingness,
your emptiness, that God can fill you with Himself. Souls of
prayer are souls of great silence.[6]

Listening to God pays off with clarity of direction and personal
comfort, as Thomas à Kempis wrote centuries ago:

Blessed is the soul who hears the Lord speaking and receives
the word of comfort from his mouth. Blessed are the ears that
receive the echoes of the soft whisper of God and aren't dis-
tracted by the murmurings of the world. Truly blessed are the
ears that listen—not to the sounds surrounding them—but to
the voice of Truth inside.[7]

Like the disciples, we can get so wrapped up on earth that
we fail to hear what heaven is saying to us. The lines of communication and openness to him are critical to receiving his
direction. Whether we are sitting silently on a rock or rocking
in a vanload of children, it seems that we will hear from God
when we are dependent on him, when we recognize that his
voice—whether it's *Stop!* or *Go!*—is essential for our very lives.

PRAYER FOR LISTENING TO GOD

*Lord, your powerful and majestic voice is heard through-
out the earth. You thunder over the earth, shaking the
desert and twisting the oaks. My prayer is to you alone,
Lord God. At just the right time and in the abundance of
your steadfast love, I know you will answer me, because*

you are good and faithful. Thank you, Lord, that you counsel me and instruct my heart. You are not far off but are always as near as my right hand. I know that I can call on you, because you not only will hear my prayer, but also will answer me. Lord, sometimes it feels as though you have forsaken me, because when I cry out, you do not answer. When trouble is near me, do not be far from me, as it seems as though there is no one to help me. There are other times, Lord, when I simply need a word from you that would point me in the right direction or stop me in my tracks for my own protection from a mistake or safety from harm. Father, please answer me when I am in distress, for I trust in the name of the Lord my God. I will listen to your voice because you are my life. Speak, Lord, for I, your servant, am listening. In Jesus' name, amen!

Adapted from Psalm 29:3–5, 7–8; 69:13; 16:7–8; 17:6; 20:1, 7;
22:1, 11; Deuteronomy 30:20; 1 Samuel 3:9

GROWING IN *Prayer*

1. Do you believe that God still speaks to believers today?

2. Read Matthew 3:17 and Mark 1:11. In the context of Jesus' baptism, what do you think the Father was trying to communicate to his Son?

3. Has there been a time in your life when you sensed God's affirmation of you? Explain the situation and how you felt.

4. At the Mount of Transfiguration the Father spoke and said, "This is my Son, whom I love. Listen to him!" (Mark 9:7). Why would God tell Peter, James, and John to listen to Jesus?

5. When would people need a pay-attention kind of message from God? Have you experienced a time in your life when you felt God gave you clear direction?

6. The third time an audible word from the Father is recorded in the gospels occurred when Jesus had returned to Jerusalem for the Passover Feast. When the Father spoke, Jesus said this was for the benefit of the others listening. What do you think he meant?

7. Is there a situation you are now going through for which you would like to hear directly from God? What kind of direction do you need?

Chapter 2

Jesus' Prayer in the Face of Temptation

Depending on how you might look at the situation, one of the best—or worst—parts of teaching in a public school could be the number of goodies in the faculty room. On Mondays folks often brought leftover homemade cookies from the weekend to cheer everyone up for the week ahead. Tuesdays were faculty meetings, and sometimes the principal would have candy on the tables. On Wednesdays—hump days, meaning we'd made it halfway through the workweek—something fun often was shared. It went downhill from there with health plan and investment salespeople bringing their bakery bribes and students doing Krispy Kreme, cookie dough, and See's Candy fund raisers. And then there were holidays, which, of course, always must be celebrated with sugary somethings.

I don't know about you, but it's hard for me to resist cute little things to eat. All sorts of temptations can derail my intent to eat the healthy foods that fuel my day for productivity rather than sluggishness. There are also many other kinds of temptations that can cause serious relational and other problems:

- Using pornography
- Drinking to excess
- Abusing prescription pain medicine
- Skipping your workout
- Reading someone else's diary
- Telling a friend what his or her problem is
- Gossiping about the boss (or another co-worker)
- Calling in sick when you are not
- Checking social media or surfing the internet while at work
- Padding an expense account (or taking home supplies from work)
- Watching television all day
- Overspending and emotional shopping
- Falling to sexual temptations
- Sleeping in—or staying up too late
- Giving in to anger and making hurtful comments
- Using curse words

Although it may seem insignificant when we give in, our weak action could also impact others and thus, the work of God. For example, calling in sick to work when I simply want a "mental health day" at home could send a signal to my children that it is okay to skip school or cheat on a test. And others—those who have not yet put their faith in Christ—can point to such actions as hypocritical and distance themselves even more from considering a commitment. Our response to temptation matters.

As we attempt to follow God's direction for our lives, temptations can significantly delay or divert us. At the beginning of Jesus' ministry, the Spirit of God led him into the desert to be tempted by the devil (Matthew 4:1). But there was a plan to face the temptations ahead. While one gospel records, "After fasting forty days and forty nights, he was hungry" (Matthew 4:2), another reports that in the wilderness, "for forty days he was tempted by the devil. He ate nothing during those days, and at the end of them he was hungry" (Luke 4:2). And while both accounts relate only three specific temptations from Satan, it can certainly be assumed that the devil did not sit back for forty days but was tempting Jesus all along. Jesus took The Test seriously. Just think: What if he had not passed The Test? What if, in his human frailty, he had caved to his hunger, quit his fast, and turned the stones to bread, as Satan had taunted him to do? He would not have been God's perfectly unspoiled gift, the Savior of mankind. Because Jesus took temptation seriously, we should, too.

Anticipate Prayerfully

Jesus taught about praying to counter temptation and modeled what to do. In fact, Jesus prepared for temptation prayerfully. Both writers recorded that Jesus fasted for those forty days. Jesus was a Jew, so he would have followed the Jewish spiritual tradition of fasting, which meant abstention from both food and drink. The Hebrews fasted on the Day of Atonement and after their exile on four other annual days, marking disasters in their history.[1] The purpose behind fasting is the pursuit of God, and so it is that prayer naturally accompanies fasting. Those who fast are seeking God's guidance and his strength, which will not necessarily be received merely through a ritualistic practice. Seeking God through prayer is the other natural strand in the two-ply cord.

Jesus readied himself for the impact of temptation with fasting and prayer. *The Message* gives insight into what Jesus would face in the desert: "Next Jesus was taken into the wild by the Spirit for the Test. The Devil was ready to give it" (Matthew 4:1).

After Christ was victorious over Satan's temptations, we learn that Satan "left him until an opportune time" (Luke 4:13). The enemy is always on the lookout for ways to trip us up.

I recently visited a friend in another state who was dog-sitting for her daughter. The safest place in the house for poochie to be confined was the kitchen, and my friend kept the place cordoned off with one of those gates used to keep toddlers off stairways. One afternoon we had picked up Chick-fil-A sandwiches for everyone, and I set mine on the kitchen table while I poured a glass of water. However, as quickly as I turned my back, poochie jumped up on the chair, snatched my chicken sandwich, and chomped the thing down. I soon found out that poochie regularly preyed on ignorant folks like me, who didn't know to keep my chair pushed in under the table. Likewise, the enemy continually looks for opportunities to make us fall to temptation. He is always ready, so we need to be, too.

Jesus also taught that we should pray not to be led into temptation. In his model prayer—the Lord's Prayer—he closed with, "And lead us not into temptation, but deliver us from the evil one" (Matthew 6:13). The Holy Spirit actually led Jesus into the desert; Jesus would not wish that on any of his followers. Praying against the pull of temptation can have great effect. If my greatest weakness is the tug of emotional shopping when others hurt or disappoint me, prayer could strengthen me so that I recognize how I'm being drawn, and then pray, *Lead me not*. Just. Say. No.

The idea of being led into temptation is curious. We would tend to think the enemy is the one responsible for all the enticements: "The devil made me do it!" We know God is not tempting us, as James 1:13 states, "No one should say, 'God is tempting me.' For God cannot be tempted by evil, nor does he tempt anyone; but each one is tempted when, by his own evil desire, he is dragged away and enticed." However, we see from Jesus' temptations in the desert and his teaching through the Lord's Prayer that God can lead us into situations in which we will be tempted. If this is so, there must be a purpose in our facing temptation. God would not want us to fail over and over. But if encountering temptation strengthens us—because we learn the habit of prayer (and even fasting)—we will draw closer to the Father because of our growing focus and dependence on him. That new, positive pattern of prayer will help us turn from that which would make us weaker and less effective. Prayerfully equipping ourselves for temptation develops the strength to say no and walk away. When Jesus fasted and prayed, he was facing Godward. Similarly, when we pray, we face Godward, not manward.[1] The act of facing Godward creates spiritual discipline.

So what would that prayer sound like? Jesus taught, "Lead me not . . ." Here are my versions:

Lead me not to the junk-food aisle.

Lead me not to that dress-for-less store, where I tend to rationalize all kinds of purchases I do not need.

Lead me not to Facebook for the tenth time today.

Jesus also said, "But deliver us from . . ." This is how we could pray strategically:

Deliver me from my addiction to sweets.

Deliver me from seeking comfort through shopping.

Deliver me from an obsessive need to respond on social media constantly, when I know I need to spend more time with you, Lord.

Temptation is inevitable, but we can face it successfully through the simplicity of prayer.

Keeping Watch

Sometimes we find that we are plunked into a situation where we might make an unwise decision. For example, you might be on a business trip and all of a sudden realize you are in a car, restaurant, or hotel room with only one other person—of the opposite sex. And what if that person is attractive, and you have had a series of arguments with your spouse? You are vulnerable and needy—and the enemy saw all these circumstances as an "opportune time" to trip you up (Luke 4:13). Jesus taught his disciples what to do to counter temptation in such a weak moment.

Just before Jesus was arrested, he went with his disciples (minus Judas, who was in the process of betraying him) to the Gethsemane garden to have quiet time with his Father. Eight of them were stationed in one spot of the garden while he took Peter, James, and John with him to another. He had a simple request of the three: "Sit here while I go over there and pray. My soul is overwhelmed with sorrow to the point of death. Stay here and keep watch with me" (Matthew 26:36, 38). The Greek word for *watch* in this use has the connotation of keeping awake; Jesus needed eyes-wide-open watchfulness from his followers. He knew his time was short, and he needed one more opportunity before his arrest to petition his Father and seek his will.

Jesus stepped away a bit to prostrate himself—offering his Father the best possible prayer a human can utter—but discovered that his disciples, who were supposed to be keeping watch, had fallen asleep. He then taught them something more about countering temptation, saying, "Could you men not keep watch with me for one hour? Watch and pray so that you will not fall into temptation. The spirit is willing, but the body is weak"

(Matthew 26:40–41). This is eyes-wide-open prayer, because we need to see what traps may lie ahead. Certainly Jesus wanted his disciples to look out and make sure no one found them too soon. However, he said, ". . . so that *you* will not fall into temptation" (emphasis added). Jesus knew not only that the disciples needed to summon strength through that long night, but also that they would have many challenging days ahead when their faith and humanness would be severely tested by those who would attempt to drag them away from being Christ followers.

Jesus also implied that his followers not be so naïve as to think that life would always be smooth sailing. Going back to the example of traveling alone, I know that even though I have a good marriage, and even though I completely trust my husband and he completely trusts me, it is simply not wise to allow oneself to be in a potentially compromising situation with someone of the opposite sex. I know I am not going to do anything to hurt my marriage—but I do not know if that other person has the same view of his marriage. Keeping our eyes wide open in a metaphorical sense is watching, which, when dovetailed with prayer, Jesus said, keeps us from falling into temptation. Our bodies are weak.

The Luke version says, "Get up and pray so that you will not fall into temptation" (Luke 22:46). Just as we like to hit the snooze button and get more sleep, the disciples felt they needed snooze time as well. The enemy was tempting them to give in to their human desires instead of standing in prayer for their Lord. Sometimes we need not only to watch and pray but also to stand—take a figurative stand against temptation. We can prayerfully ask for God's deliverance from a temptation, but we also can pray aloud, "I am taking a stand against temptation to gossip about my co-worker." Words spoken aloud are powerful. In the same way your spoken words about your faith story can have an impact on others, your spoken words taking a stand against temptation are a declaration that you are looking

Godward, not manward, or inward. Those spoken words are like an army captain shouting, "Charge!" They indicate that you are aware, you are ready, you are taking a stand, and you are praying for deliverance.

Christ warned that temptation would be a woe to the world (Matthew 18:7–9). He said temptation is inevitable and that it will bring pain and trouble to mankind. His model to us is not just prayer but also fasting, which while not so common in Christian circles today, is still very powerful in bringing about God's work on earth. Author Elmer L. Towns advocates the practice of fasting for spiritual breakthrough.

> If you are serious enough about the personal and social tasks before you as a Christian to take up the discipline of fasting, you can expect resistance. Interference and opposition. Plan for it, insofar as you are able. Do not be caught unawares. Remember that you are attempting to advance in your spiritual journey and to gain ground for the Kingdom. That necessitates taking ground away from the enemy—and no great movement of the Holy Spirit goes unchallenged by the enemy.[3]

Towns suggests seeking out a committed prayer partner for your times of fasting, to consult a physician in advance to make sure you can do this, and to fast for only one day at a time.[4]

Some have found that prayer in tandem with fasting can break the power of certain temptations in their lives. Not spending time fixing food and eating it but instead praying and seeking God in his Word can break a hold of temptation over you. Fourteen years ago I found myself addicted to prescription pain medication. After caring for my son who'd had knee surgery, and lifting both his ice and his movement machines over and over, I suffered from what the emergency room neurologist said was the worst herniated disc he had ever seen. I tried to suffer through the pain for three weeks, flat in bed, unable to move or even lift my head. Desperate, I went ahead with surgery, which was successful, but after two more weeks on the pain meds, I realized I was counting down the minutes until my next pill. I began fasting and praying for release from the physiological addiction, and then it seemed God nudged me to take only half a pill for the doses the next day and then quit entirely the day after that. When I followed through with this plan and got off the meds completely, I found I actually had no pain at all.

You see, with the temptations that swirl around us, we often have ourselves convinced we have to have the Whatever. A want becomes a need, and we weaken, thinking we have no power to overcome that woe of the world. Jesus, our Master Teacher, however, has shown us we can overcome temptation through the practice of prayer, which is always the best approach to problem solving.

PRAYER TO OVERCOME TEMPTATION

Lord, I am weak and fall to temptation in the area of
_____. *Even though your Son's sacrifice provides grace and mercy for all believers, I do not want to sin anymore and thus continue to challenge that measure of grace and mercy from you. Lead me not to this temptation, Lord, but instead deliver me from that evil practice. I do not want to let this sin reign in my body and do not want to follow its evil desires, thus making me fall and damaging my testimony about your work in my life. When I face temptation, help me not to offer the parts of my body to sin as instruments of disobedience but instead offer myself to you as an instrument of righteousness. I proclaim that sin shall not be my master, because I have been set free from sin. I understand that no temptation can*

seize me except what is common to people, but that you are faithful and will not allow me to be tempted beyond what I am able to withstand. Instead, I can look for your way of escape from that temptation so that I can win over it. Because I know that putting myself in compromising situations where temptation is more likely to occur is unhealthy, I will avoid those situations and choose healthy alternatives. Thus, I will not give the enemy a foothold in my life. With your spiritual armor of truth, righteousness, the gospel of peace, faith, your Word, and prayer, I know I can win this battle. In Jesus' name, amen!

Adapted from Matthew 6:13; Romans 6;
1 Corinthians 10:13–14; Ephesians 4:27; 6:10–20

GROWING IN *Prayer*

1. What temptations typically tend to trip you up?

2. Why is it important not to give in to temptation? How would giving in affect others?

3. How did Jesus prepare for and battle temptation in the wilderness?

4. Why do you think Jesus' model prayer in Matthew 6:13 includes "And lead us not into temptation, but deliver us from the evil one"?

5. The author says that when we pray, we are facing Godward, not manward. What do you think this means? How could facing Godward help us handle temptation?

6. What does watching have to do with praying, in regard to temptation? (See Matthew 26:40–41.)

7. As you think again about the kinds of temptations that trip you up, how could you pray to resist them?

Chapter 3

Jesus' Prayer for Daily Needs

As a teacher, I was always misplacing my keys. Those occasions reminded me of a story my mother, who also was a teacher, often told. As a young mother, she had gotten to the point of frustration and worry one day because she couldn't find her keys. They weren't in her purse, where she always left them; they weren't on the kitchen counter or the table or her dresser; they hadn't slipped underneath the cushions of the couch or chair; and they weren't on the floor anywhere—she had gotten down on her knees and checked all the way through the house. She sat down on the edge of her bed, put her head down, and prayed, "Lord, please help me find those keys."

Almost instantly she felt moved to run her hand down the side of the mattress to a spot where it lay atop the box spring . . . and pulled out the keys. Some little monkey—maybe me—had stuck them there, perhaps when that monkey realized she might be in a whole bunch of trouble for taking Mommy's keys.

Prayer seems to come naturally in times of crisis. However, while we have prayers of Jesus from his times of need, it's interesting that when he teaches the disciples how to pray, he offers one that speaks to the daily-ness of life: the Lord's Prayer.

> "This, then, is how you should pray:
>
> "'Our Father in heaven,
> hallowed be your name.
> your kingdom come,
> your will be done
>   on earth as it is in heaven.
> Give us today our daily bread.
> Forgive us our debts,
>   as we also have forgiven our debtors.
> And lead us not into temptation,
>   but deliver us from the evil one.'"
>
> Matthew 6:9–13

The prayer is part of a larger teaching about prayer and other spiritual practices as a whole.

There are two ways to teach: One is through direct teaching, and the other is by modeling the behavior or technique. For example, as a high school English teacher, when I was teaching a basic paragraph form used for argumentation, I would tell my students exactly how each sentence in the paragraph should function. But I also would give them samples of real paragraphs so they could see how to execute one themselves. I *told* them how, then *showed* them how. Fiction writers know this as the difference between *telling* language and *showing* language.

When Jesus offered the model prayer, he was showing the disciples how to pray in response to one of the disciples' requests: "Lord, teach us to pray, just as John taught his disciples" (Luke 11:1). In other words, he gave them a basic sample prayer—a formula or an outline for prayer. But the disciple's question came right after Jesus had been teaching about prayer. As an educator reading this again recently, I chuckled as I remembered well how I could spend twenty minutes explaining how to do something, only to be followed up by a student's question, "Now, what do we do?" What that student wanted—and what the disciples wanted—was a sample. Just as I would say in the classroom, "Okay, your first paragraph could sound like . . . ," the disciples wanted to know what a *prayer* could sound like. And just as I would not mean for my students to copy my example verbatim, Jesus also was giving the disciples a sample of what they could say and most likely did not intend for them to copy his prayer exactly.

This raises questions. Why didn't they know how to pray? Hadn't they heard prayers at home and in the temple? Hadn't they read the psalms, which is a series of prayers? The thing is, Jesus was completely mixing things up in the religious world. Whereas Jews were to follow the letter of the law, Jesus taught the spirit of it. This new attitude is brought out in the text just prior to the Lord's Prayer.

> "And when you pray, do not be like the hypocrites, for they love to pray standing in the synagogues and on the street corners to be seen by men. I tell you the truth, they have received their reward in full. But when you pray, go into your room, close the door and pray to your Father, who is unseen. Then your Father, who sees what is done in secret, will reward you. And when you pray, do not keep on babbling like pagans, for they think they will be heard because of their many words. Do not be like them, for your Father knows what you need before you ask him."
>
> Matthew 6:5–8

Secret and Simple

Jesus laid out two important teachings here about prayer in this chunk that Matthew included in his account of the Sermon on the Mount—and these both relate to the content of the Lord's Prayer. First, he taught believers to pray privately. He had observed the hypocrisy of the religious leaders of his time who flaunted their devotional practices for the approval of men. He introduced this discourse by teaching his listeners not to parade their acts of supposed righteousness in front of others. "You will have no reward from your Father in heaven," he said (Matthew 6:1). He also said not to announce acts of generosity to the needy but instead to not "let your left hand know what your right hand is doing, so that your giving may be in secret" (Matthew 6:3–4). Giving should be for the sake of the needy alone—not to score points with others. Jesus taught that if giving is done so as to impress others, the givers have enough of a reward, and he implied that the Father rewards only those who give with the right attitude (Matthew 6:2, 4). This ties to the teaching on praying privately. Jesus saw that hypocrites prayed publicly on street corners solely for the praise of men, not for the purpose of communicating with the Father. Prayer is an intimate expression of our heart—its attitude and its needs—that best is related in a private setting behind closed doors.

The classic example of someone who sought privacy in prayer was Susanna Wesley—the mother of nineteen children, two of whom were Charles and John, who is credited with founding the Methodist Church. Because she needed privacy for her prayer time but had none in such a lively household, she would throw her apron over her head—a sign the children took that Mother was praying and not to disturb her.[1] The modern classic comes from the recent film *War Room*, in which the elder character, Miss Clara, has a literal prayer closet lined with prayer requests and Scripture references—a practice that actress Priscilla Shirer (portraying Elizabeth Stallings) adopts to save her marriage, which it does.[2] In both these cases, while others might know that prayer was underway, the conversation itself would be private—and certainly not for the praise of men. For another illustration, if you mailed someone a letter, others might know the letter was being sent, but you most likely would not read its contents aloud so they could laud your language.

One notable exception is that prayer in a corporate setting of worship is not only appropriate but right and good. Every one of the four gospel writers recorded that Jesus was upset when he found vendors and money changers at the temple in Jerusalem at the time of the Passover. In fact, he overturned their tables, declaring, "It is written, 'My house will be called a house of prayer,' but you are making it a 'den of robbers'" (Matthew 21:13). Praying (with music or without it) by oneself or with others in a place of worship, then, is something good indeed.

Jesus' other teaching in Matthew 6 prior to the Lord's Prayer is that prayer should be simple. God is not impressed with a long-winded dissertation from the pray-er—the succinct request is enough. In fact, he taught that pagans babbled on and on because they thought that longwindedness would win their argument. The believer does not need to babble at God because our Father already knows our heart, knows our need, and knows what we will say before we even speak it. The case with God is not won with an onslaught of words. Short and sweet is enough.

At this point it seems the disciples were confused. All they'd heard were hypocrites trying to impress others on the street corner with their holier-than-thou posture and impressive-sounding language, as well as babblers in the courts trying to win their case. So one of them asked Jesus to teach them how to pray, and the Master Teacher demonstrated in response.

A Perfect Example

Such refreshment is this prayer! He lets us off the hook. We don't have to be wordy or pompous. We don't have to be impressive.

In fact, we can't impress him at all because he knows our attitude and knows our need before we even ask. What a relief this model prayer is, given in just six simple parts: the address, the posture, the hope, the request, the covenant, and the plea.

The Address

The prayer's salutation—"Our Father in heaven"—clearly lays out the relationship between the person praying and the Father. This opening puts into perspective that our Father is to be honored and is worthy of our worship. He is in heaven, above all people and things. He is greater than any concern on earth. He is the Creator of the universe. Jesus also uses the word *our* here. The Father is not just Jesus' Father; he is Father of all who believe in him. He is my Father, and he is your Father. He can be approached by all who put their faith in him. Christianity is different from any other faith because it is all about having a personal relationship with our Father God through Jesus Christ.

The Posture

While the address establishes the relationship, the next statement relates the posture we should have while approaching the God of the universe: "hallowed be your name." Even if we are not literally on our knees in a physical state of reverence, we should understand that God is holy and worthy of our awe. The word *hallow* comes from the Greek *hagiazō*, which means "to make holy . . . to set apart for God, to sanctify."[3] That which is hallowed is the opposite of that which is common. One Bible version reads, "Pray along these lines: 'Our Father in heaven, we honor your holy name'" (Matthew 6:9 TLB). God's name throughout the Bible is revered, so much so that the Hebrew name for God, Yahweh, was rendered the unpronounceable and unspoken YHWH. It was too holy to put into finite language or utterance. Jesus taught his disciples and teaches us today that while God is close at hand and is as approachable as a father, he is to be revered and honored.

The Hope

Why do we pray at all? Simply, life is challenging, and we need help. We need to know we're not alone. We need life to be different, to be better. We don't have answers, and so we go to the Father with our heavy hearts. In other words, we pray because we have hope—so I've called the next section of the Lord's Prayer *The Hope*: "your kingdom come, your will be done on earth as it is in heaven" (Matthew 6:10). There are two parts to the hope. The first clause asks for God to bring about his kingdom on earth—the final, Jesus-is-back celebration. What a glorious day that will be! No more worries, no more cares, no more cancer, no more tax-return-due-tomorrow. Just life with Jesus. The second clause is the until-then clause. Something like this:

Until then, Lord, may your will be done on earth.

Until then, Father, could you please do what you know is best, despite my humanness, despite my mistakes?

Until then, God, would you work through the circumstances of my life in this mixed-up world and be glorified through it all?

Jesus prayed such a prayer in the Upper Room before his walk to the cross—which we will look at in more depth in chapter 10—another Jesus prayer, and so, a good one indeed.

The Request

I love how Eugene Peterson translated Matthew 6:11 in *The Message*: "Keep us alive with three square meals." Jesus teaches us here to pray for the daily things—bread, shelter, clothing. In other words, the necessities that would sustain life, not the luxuries. In Jesus' time the bread he would have eaten was a simple food, a small loaf or cake made from flour and water and baked into an oblong or round shape as thick as the thumb. Bread was not sliced but broken into pieces.[4] For food, he was dependent upon the disciples' fishing catch, as well as the generosity of others to provide the daily bread, which could include food in general, but might in actuality have been nothing more than bread. Richard Foster, author and founder of Renovaré, writes that we should not demean these simple petitions for daily needs—that viewing other forms of prayer as more enlightened is a false spirituality. "Petition, then, is not a lower form of prayer. It is our staple diet."[5]

It's interesting that Jesus said, "Give *us* today our *daily* bread" (Matthew 6:11, emphases added). He includes the whole group of disciples along with himself when he says "us." And he asks for "daily" bread—just what they'll need for sustenance for the day. What do you need for today? *Need* is the operative word here. Do you need a working vehicle? Pray for God to provide the car that will get you from here to there and back. Do you need a job? Pray for your Father to make the connection. Do you need a house you can afford? Pray for God to point you in the right direction for something that meets your needs but stays within your budget. God will provide for your needs. He may choose to bless you above and beyond what you have requested, but notice that we don't see Jesus asking for the accoutrements of wealth.

The Covenant

The next section of the Lord's Prayer seems to be a form of covenant or contract. The Lord himself introduced the concept of a contract in the Old Testament books. He covenanted with Noah and his descendants not to send another earth-destroying flood (Genesis 9:8–17). He gave land to Abram (Genesis 15:9–21), and he promised David to establish and maintain the Davidic line on the throne of Israel (2 Samuel 7:5–16). Another agreement or covenant of sorts is found in the Lord's Prayer: "Forgive us our debts, as we also have forgiven our debtors" (Matthew 6:12). With this, Jesus instructs us not only to ask God for forgiveness for our sins, but also to forgive others who may have offended us, hurt us, or treated us unfairly. We should not take this contract or covenant lightly, as the God who forgives also expects us to forgive others. Jesus' prayer relating to forgiveness will be discussed more extensively in chapter 11, but here in the Lord's Prayer we see that we have a responsibility in prayer to fulfill a covenant and forgive if we expect forgiveness for ourselves.

The Plea

The greatest battle on earth is against Satan, who would love for us to fall to temptation and thus fail in our testimony as believers. Jesus' model prayer, though, shows us that we can ask the Father to spare us from temptations, to help us resist those things that would trip us up, and to rescue and save us from the enemy. The Greek *rhuomai* for *deliver* here has the sense that we can ask to be taken away from temptation,[6] so I think today we might say, "Get me out of here!" The battle also may be with our own weaknesses, as is implied in *The Message*: "Keep us safe from ourselves and the Devil" (Matthew 6:13 MESSAGE). Recognizing that we need help to battle temptation is the first step in conquering it.

I grew up reciting the Lord's Prayer in church and at home. During those years it may have been rote, but today it has great meaning to me, mostly because it reminds me that prayer is not complicated. Jesus made it so simple that even uneducated fishermen could confidently approach their heavenly Father and spell out their simple requests.

The past few months have been really rewarding to me because I've been mentoring the youngest of our four children, Bethany, as she took on her first assignment as an English teacher for high school juniors and seniors. Here's the gist of one of our conversations:

"Mom, I am starting a unit on screenwriting with my creative writing class. So what would you do first?"

[After raising my dropped jaw . . .] "Tell them to develop their characters first."

"Okay, and what will they do to develop them?"

"Tell them to start with a strong protagonist who has a quest for good stakes—a good purpose for the common good. Bring in an antagonist who wants the same thing but for evil intent. Then go from there."

"Sounds good. Now what will I say, Mom?

Three hours later the conversation from here to Honolulu ended. I would love to have been a fly on that classroom wall to watch and listen to my daughter teach her students, not even ten years younger than she is. And I picture Jesus watching over his children today, learning from his model prayer and trying their best to put into words their basic, simple needs to their heavenly Father.

Prayer is a simple confession of faith—that God exists and listens and answers. Some might say that they are "just not good at prayer." A friend recently mentioned this to me as we sat in a restaurant for lunch. I smiled and said, "But you just ordered exactly what you wanted from the menu. You know what you need—just mention that to your heavenly Father." Just today I got a message from a friend, a former teacher, asking me to pray for her husband, who had a sudden illness and was flown to the hospital, where doctors could not diagnose his problem. Though she and I had never had a conversation about faith, we had been Facebook friends for many years; she knew I prayed and had noticed I coordinated a weekly prayer meeting on Facebook. Her request touched me—that she would trust me to pray for their daily bread, which that day was their basic need for his health. Jesus reminds us through the Lord's Prayer that taking our needs to the Father is not a complicated affair. Our simple words with our simply humbled attitude are all we need to make the prayer perfect.

PRAYER FOR DAILY NEEDS

Father, thank you that through me you provide for all my daily needs: food, a place to live, clothing, health, and purpose for my life through meaningful work. Send a blessing, Lord, on my work and home. As I delight in you and your Word, I do feel like a tree planted by streams of waters because of the abundance around me. We who seek you, Lord, lack no good thing—so I trust you for your care for my family and me. You heal us and rescue us when we need you. Thank you that you promise to bring health and healing to our lives, so that our lives are lived out purposefully. Lord, I want to be wise about my finances and plan carefully. Your Word says that whoever loves money is never satisfied. I do not want to be a lover of money, Lord, but instead someone who seeks you and your priorities for my family and me. Help me get my priorities straightened out and give me the wisdom to find solutions to needs. Show me how to serve you alone—not money—so that I am a good example to others and so that you are honored through me. In Jesus' name, amen!

Adapted from Deuteronomy 8:18; 28:8,11;
Psalm 1:3; 34:10; 107:20; Jeremiah 30:17; 2 John 2;
Matthew 14:28–30; Romans 13:8; 1 Thessalonians 2:9;
2 Thessalonians 3:6–10; Matthew 6:19–34

GROWING IN *Prayer*

1. Do you pray for daily needs? If not, why?

2. Jesus taught about prayer and modeled how to pray. Which method touches you more personally and why?

3. Jesus teaches us not to pray on "street corners." When would it be all right to pray publicly?

4. Where do you pray? Do you feel it is quiet enough for your prayer time?

5. Read Matthew 6:7–8. How do you feel about praying with simple, concise words? Do you think prayer language should be different from everyday language?

6. What were the six different parts of the Lord's Prayer identified in this chapter?

7. Which parts of the Lord's Prayer reflect how you typically pray?

8. How might your prayer life for daily things change after reading this chapter?

Chapter 4

Jesus' Prayer of Praise

In most circumstances I am not at a loss for words. All of my professional jobs have revolved around them. Technical writer/editor: making sense out of computerese for proposals for multimillion-dollar government contracts. Daily newspaper reporter: covering the city and cops beat. City editor: choosing stories off the wires and fashioning headlines that catch the reader's eye. Paralegal: drafting court and other documents. High school English teacher: teaching students to analyze and to write. And then there's the professional communicator side of me.

However, when filled with joy—such as recent occasions at the rim of the Grand Canyon or within the solid rock canyon at Zion National Park or at an overlook of Bryce Canyon or underneath a fifty-foot stone arch at Arches National Park—all I could say was "Wow, God." Just wow. My eyes danced from one piece of red rock gorgeousness to the next on our trip to the Southwest. As Craig drove along, I'd joke, "Well, there you are, Utah, showing off again." But my heart was filling up and spilling over into quiet praise for the Maker of not only that corner of America, but also all earthly creation.

There may be some confusion about what exactly praise as a form of prayer is—perhaps partly because many people call contemporary Christian music *praise* music. While some of it does praise God, much of it is actually reflective in nature, convicting us to have better heart attitudes or even reminding us simply to breathe or to rest or to sing. Prayers of praise lead to the worship of our Lord God.

I often overlook the practice of praise in my life. Maybe you do, too. I'm sort of a just-do-it kind of girl who lives to check off items on to-do lists and to wipe off calendar obligations from the hallway whiteboard. I will intercede for others immediately when asked. I pray for all needs God puts in front of my eyes. My older neighbor was taken by ambulance last night and then Care-Flighted away. I prayed long into the night. But often I forget to stop and praise my good, good Father.

Jesus taught us to praise God in the Lord's Prayer, but there was another occasion when he offered praise. The opposition was heating up against Jesus. His cousin John the Baptist was in prison. The cities where he had performed miracle after miracle were unrepentant. And he was not welcomed in Samaria. Nonetheless, one day his followers returned to him with good news from their travels to tell others about Jesus, and we see his prayer-filled response:

> At that time Jesus, full of joy through the Holy Spirit, said, "I praise you, Father, Lord of heaven and earth, because you have hidden these things from the wise and learned, and revealed them to little children. Yes, Father, for this was your good pleasure."
>
> Luke 10:21

Jesus had sent out the thirty-six pairs. He had instructed them to travel lightly and told them what to say when entering a home. He had taught them to heal the sick and what to do if they were not welcomed. And yet, when the followers returned with great results, he didn't pat himself on the back or even tell them "Good job!" Instead, he gave praise to his Father.

Praise should be an essential part of our praying lives—as a spontaneous and natural reaction to life's circumstances, but also as a personal discipline in our prayer-closet times. Willow Creek pastor Bill Hybels writes, "Worship God and praise him when you come to him in prayer."[1] Our praise is our one-man-band worship time, whether we're singing or not. To praise God is to glorify him by attributing to him those characteristic perfections of his.[2] We acknowledge the holy character of God: his faithfulness, his love, his goodness, and so on. In Jesus' prayer he praised his Father for his sovereignty—the plan to keep the truth about who Jesus was hidden from the religious leaders and instead to reveal it to "little children"—the less-than-influential people of the towns where Jesus and his disciples traveled. He praised God for his "good pleasure"—his will to effect the perfect plan for salvation to come to the world through the life and death of his son Jesus. So one purpose of praise is to acknowledge the holy character of God.

Position and Posture

Another thing this short prayer of Jesus does is reinforce in a believer's mind the relationship between God and man. He showed this in his prayer when he prayed, "I praise you, Father, Lord of heaven and earth. . . ." Just as he prayed in the Lord's Prayer, Jesus called God "Father" and established that his Father was the Lord of all things. Prayer puts us in our place—God above, and us below. He is Lord everlasting; we are created beings whose lives on earth are subject to his plan. Yes, our lives are eternal—subject to one direction or the other, by our choice—but the extent of our physical lives is in his hands. Good students do not make arrogant demands of their teachers; they respect and demonstrate respect for those classroom figures of authority. Praise should put into perspective who God is as we pray, and thus influence the way we pray.

We also see from our Master Teacher that praise is a natural response to joy. Luke wrote that Jesus was "full of joy through the Holy Spirit" (Luke 10:21). Inspired by joy, appreciation, and the love God has for us, our hearts, spirits, and minds return love to the Father through praise. Richard Foster writes that praise is one of two forms of adoration—thanksgiving being the other. While in thanksgiving we express appreciation for what God has done for us, in praise we give thanks for who God is. Period. Foster writes that adoration is

> the spontaneous yearning of the heart to worship, honor, magnify, and bless God.
>
> In one sense adoration is not a special form of prayer, for all true prayer is saturated with it. It is the air in which prayer breathes, the sea in which prayer swims. In another sense, though, it *is* distinct from other kinds of prayer, for in adoration we enter the rarefied air of selfless devotion. We ask for nothing but to cherish him. We seek nothing but his exaltation. We focus on nothing but his goodness. "In the prayer of adoration we love God for himself, for his very being, for his radiant joy."[3]

Praise isn't kissing up to God. It isn't buttering him up before we lay on the heavy pleading. There is no ulterior motive. Our praise is a simple offering—the best gift we can give to God other than our obedience. The lovely thing is, though, that praise can transform us.

The practice of praise helps us agree with God. Our words of worship might actually change our mindset about what we think we need. Instead of looking at prayer from the point of our to-do list, praise focuses us upwards. Author Ole Hallesby writes that "when we worship or give praise, we give God glory for what He is in Himself," with "self-forgetting adoration, seeing and praising only the majesty and power of God, His grace and redemption."[4] Praise is a mind-shift from a focus on self to a reminder of God's character and perspective. That new perspective, then, could change not only *how* we pray, but also *for what* we pray. For example, if I were headed into prayer with a woe-is-me attitude about a friend's unkind remark, but then remember to start that prayer with praise about God's mysterious yet perfect ways, I might instead thank him for the new challenge in my life that would be used to sand the rough edges of my character. That prayerful change of perspective may be part of what Paul meant when he wrote,

> Do not conform any longer to the pattern of this world, but be transformed by the renewing of your mind. Then you will be able to test and approve what God's will is—his good, pleasing and perfect will.
>
> Romans 12:2

As we grow in our love for God and worship him more through prayer, our understanding of his will for our lives will also grow and help us pray more in accord with his will.

Making a Mental Switch

Okay, so let's just face the fact that there are many times when life is not fun. We may not be having a peace-like-a-river/love-like-an-ocean/joy-like-a-fountain kind of day at all. In fact, we might even be mad at God for the moment . . . or week

. . . or season of life. It's hard to summon *whoohoo!* when you're caregiving for an elderly parent or when you're staring at divorce papers or when your last paycheck was six months ago. When writer Becky Harling was diagnosed with cancer ten years ago, she begged God for healing. However, a friend challenged her instead to spend twenty minutes a day praising God, a practice that she says brought transformative joy into her life.[5]

I experienced the same changes in my own life when I started prayerwalking. The depression that had clouded most of my adult life lifted. Irrational fears about what might happen in my family's life or mine disappeared. I knew I was different when my son Joshua found me in the kitchen one morning before school.

"Mom, what are you doing?" he asked.

I looked down, and then at him. It seemed obvious to me. "Making peanut butter and jelly sandwiches?"

He shook his head. "No, Mom, you were singing!" And he walked away shaking his head.

You see, he'd never heard his mother singing that early in the morning. The grouchy, *I-said-get-up* mom had a different perspective because she had spent an hour that morning seeking God's face in the practice of prayerwalking.[6]

But the idea of praise isn't part of a self-improvement strategy. It's not meant to be prayerlifting—like a huge weight of something else to carry . . . or drag. I think it can be more of a mental switch if we think of Jesus' "Our Father in heaven, hallowed be your name" (Matthew 6:9). This just-do-it girl has learned that it helps to become strategic and intentional about incorporating more praise in my prayer. One way is to choose a characteristic of God that seems relevant to my perspective, so I devised a chart to help you also to develop your praise vocabulary and see how your praise might connect to whatever you are experiencing.

DAY	CHARACTERISTIC OF GOD	PRAY WHEN . . .
1	Loving	. . . you don't feel lovable.
2	Creative	. . . the beauty of nature stuns you.
3	Sovereign	. . . life is confusing.
4	Patient	. . . you mess up . . . again.
5	Faithful	. . . life is hard.
6	Wise	. . . you are not sure which path to take.
7	Protective	. . . you feel threatened.
8	Redeeming	. . . tragedy strikes and you need hope.
9	Honorable	. . . you need assurance of his promises.
10	Good	. . . you see his care for you.
11	Compassionate	. . . you feel sad.
12	All-powerful	. . . a situation needs his intervention.
13	Just	. . . injustice strikes.
14	Never-changing	. . . life is tenuous and you need stability.
15	Reliable	. . . you need to know God will come through.
16	Trustworthy	. . . others around you fail you.
17	Freeing	. . . you feel trapped.
18	Infallible	. . . you need to know truth stands.
19	Alive	. . . you question his existence.
20	Comforting	. . . you are hurting.
21	Merciful	. . . you have sinned.
22	Holy	. . . the world is ugly around you.
23	Generous	. . . you are in need.
24	Victorious	. . . you are battling something dark.
25	Ever-present	. . . you need a steady guide.
26	Truthful	. . . you are not sure what is right.
27	Grace-giving	. . . you make a mistake.
28	Infinite	. . . it feels as though life is falling apart.
29	All-sufficient	. . . you feel ill-equipped.
30	All-knowing	. . . you need to know he understands.
31	Worthy	. . . you want to do better.

A Day 1 prayer could look like this:

Lord, you are my loving God. You fashioned me in my mother's womb. You have pursued a relationship with me and speak to me through your Word. You have loved me with long-suffering kindness, despite my frailties and mistakes. I honor and worship you, Father, for you are my loving God Most High.

It need not be long-winded or complicated, as we learned in the last chapter. No matter if our praise is spontaneous in reaction to something amazing that has happened or more purposefully planned as with our daily prayers, praise will develop our awe-filled respect for our Maker and transform our hearts—and perhaps even our prayers.

PRAYER OF PRAISE

I praise you, Father, Lord of heaven and earth, because you sovereignly orchestrate the moments and circumstances of my life. You are a good, good Father because you want the best for me and guide me in that way. You are not only the Lord of heaven and earth, you are my Lord—my rock, my fortress, and my deliverer. When life seems to crumble, I praise you nonetheless because you are my shield, my stronghold, and the horn of my salvation. I know you are my protector and are reliable and worthy of my faith and trust. When I am confused, I know that your way is perfect and that your Word is flawless. The heavens declare your glory, God. I speak of your faithfulness: Just as your sun rises in the east and sets in the west, I know I can trust that you will be with me. In a world that is uncertain and fickle, you are never-changing, all-sufficient, and ever-present. You are my light and my safe place. I praise your name, holy God, and delight in the fact that I will dwell in the house of the Lord all the days of my life.

Adapted from Psalm 18:2, 30; 19:1; 27:1, 4

GROWING IN *Prayer*

1. How do you incorporate praise in your times of prayer?
2. Read Luke 10:21–22. Why did Jesus offer the prayer of praise?
3. What characteristic(s) of the Father was Jesus implying in his prayer?
4. How could our prayers of praise teach us about our relationship with God?
5. How is praise a response of love?
6. How could praise transform us and influence how we pray?
7. Write and share a short prayer of praise based on one of the characteristics of God in the praise vocabulary chart.

Chapter 5

Jesus' Prayer of Thanksgiving

When I was laid off from my job in my fourth year of teaching, I was an emotional mess. I particularly remember one of the last faculty meetings when the principal was listing all of the wonderful changes that were expected for the next year. I thought, *Wonderful changes? But I won't be here!* Just before my emotions spilled out, I left the room abruptly, then burst into tears outside the building. *Why, God?* Yes, I knew God wanted me to be thankful. Yes, I knew all about 1 Thessalonians 5:16–18: "Be joyful always; pray continually; give thanks in all circumstances, for this is God's will for you in Christ Jesus." Yes, I knew my layoff was God's will. But in the midst of the mess, it was hard to be thankful. However, I would learn to embrace that kind of prayer soon after.

Jesus gave thanks in a tough time as well. In the context of the death of one of his closest friends, Lazarus, Jesus gave thanks . . . but he wept as well (see the story in John 11:1–44). He was on the other side of the Jordan River from Bethany when he heard that Lazarus was sick. Even though Lazarus's sisters, Mary and Martha, sent for Jesus, he delayed for two days before making the trip of twenty miles or so. Despite the disciples' objections to traveling back into Judea, where the Jews had tried to stone Jesus, he insisted on going, saying, "Our friend Lazarus has fallen asleep; but I am going there to wake him up" (v. 11). "Fallen asleep" is a euphemism for *died*, but the disciples did not get the subtlety, so he added, "Lazarus is dead, and for your sake I am glad I was not there, so that you may believe. But let us go to him" (v. 14). This may seem like a cruelty. Today if a doctor delayed treatment, we would be crying *malpractice*!

Two days later they arrived in Bethany, only to find that Lazarus had been in the tomb for four days. Both of the sisters separately told Jesus that if he had been there, their brother would not have died. They believed in the Healer. There was an interesting dynamic falling into place. Jesus knew his friend was dying, yet he delayed his trip so Lazarus would be even more dead, in others' eyes. We now know that he was at the threshold of yet another miracle—one seemingly even greater than raising the widow's son (Luke 7:11–15) or Jairus's daughter (Luke 8:41–42, 49–56), people whose bodies had not yet reached the tomb, people others could argue were indeed just asleep. No one was going to dispute that Lazarus had died. In fact, Martha said there would be a bad odor after they rolled away the tomb's stone. As the narrator of *A Christmas Carol* by Charles Dickens says about the deceased Marley's state, "There was no doubt whatever about that." Marley and Lazarus were dead.

While Jesus knew that there was a greater plan in this family's agony over his friend's death, and that he would raise Lazarus from the dead, his humanity took over for a spell. When Jesus approached Mary and saw her and a whole company of Jews weeping, "he was deeply moved in spirit and troubled." We understand why Jesus was deeply moved, but *troubled*? This is the same word used a chapter later (John 12:27), when Jesus was faced with the eventuality of his own death on the cross. However, the idea of death *is* troubling. It means separation from earthly loved ones. It implies physical pain of some kind. And it is an emotional earth-shaker for those left behind, which Jesus had seen in Lazarus's sisters. So when Jesus asked where Lazarus was laid and they said, "Come and see, Lord," we have the shortest but most moving sentence in Scripture: "Jesus wept" (John 11:35).

After the group arrived at the tomb and rolled the stone away, we find one of the most curious of Jesus' prayers. Jesus looked up and said,

> "Father, I thank you that you have heard me. I knew that you always hear me, but I said this for the benefit of the people standing here, that they may believe that you have sent me."

> John 11:41–42

In this short prayer we see no prayer for healing of the man who had lain dead for four days. Just a simple thank-you in advance. This could be interpreted either as presumptuous or faith-filled. It reminds me of when I write business letters and close with "Thank you for your anticipated, prompt reply." Undeniably, Jesus' delay was thus explained with his remark about the healing being for the benefit of the believers-in-the-making.

Big, Bold Prayers for the Kingdom

The other case where we see Jesus giving a prayer of thanks is in a daily-bread situation. After Jesus did a three-day healing session on a mountainside near the Sea of Galilee, he knew the four thousand (plus women and children) were without food and hungry. The disciples gathered seven loaves of bread and a few small fish.

He told the crowd to sit down on the ground. Then he took the seven loaves and the fish, and when he had given thanks, he broke them and gave them to the disciples, and they in turn to the people. They all ate and were satisfied. Afterward the disciples picked up seven basketfuls of broken pieces that were left over.

Matthew 15:35–37

Did Jesus give thanks for the seven loaves and the few small fish? Or was he—as with the miracle of raising Lazarus—giving thanks for what *would* happen? Both, I think.

There is a symbiotic relationship between faith and prayer. Jesus knew the Father would answer—and his prayer in Lazarus's healing is one of thanksgiving in advance. When he fed the four thousand plus extras, he gave thanks not only for what was in his disciples' hands at the moment, but also for the food that would be the product of the multiplication miracle. He prayed for what was, and he prayed for what would be. He also taught about this relationship between faith and prayer several times.

The first instance is in a peculiar context. He and the disciples were on their way back to Jerusalem from Bethany, where they had spent the night after the triumphal entry—most likely at Mary, Martha, and Lazarus's home. When he found no fruit on a fig tree along the way, he cursed it, and it immediately withered. When the disciples asked why, he said,

"I tell you the truth, if you have faith and do not doubt, not only can you do what was done to the fig tree, but also you can say to this mountain, 'Go, throw yourself into the sea,' and it will be done. If you believe, you will receive whatever you ask for in prayer.'"

Matthew 21:21–22

This echoes what he had taught after healing the demon-possessed boy. The disciples had tried and couldn't, and asked him why. He said,

"Because you have so little faith. I tell you the truth, if you have faith as small as a mustard seed, you can say to this mountain, 'Move from here to there' and it will move. Nothing will be impossible for you."

Matthew 17:20–21

Faith isn't a requisite for prayer, but it has a connection with receiving what was requested.

God loves big, bold prayers when they will grow his kingdom. We see that in the bold prayer of thanksgiving for the resurrection of Lazarus. But we also see this in a teaching following Luke's version of the Lord's Prayer in Luke 11:5–8. I'll give Jesus' analogy. Suppose it's midnight and you and the children are already in bed with the door locked. All of a sudden you hear a pounding on your front door and recognize your neighbor's voice. "Hey, neighbor, I'm sorry to bother you, but a friend on a journey just stopped by, and I don't have a thing to feed him. Can you help me out?" While the sleepy man in Jesus' story at first grumbles a bit, he finally gets up and gives his neighbor his dinner leftovers and more—not because the guy is the best of neighbors, but because the man's boldness struck him. Then Jesus provided the analysis about boldness and faith in prayer:

"So I say to you: Ask and it will be given to you; seek and you will find; knock and the door will be opened to you. For everyone who asks receives; he who seeks finds, and to him who knocks, the door will be opened.

"Which of you fathers, if your son asks for a fish, will give him a snake instead? Or if he asks for an egg, will give him a scorpion? If you then, though you are evil, know how to give good gifts to your children, how much more will your Father in heaven give the Holy Spirit to those who ask him!"

Luke 11:9–13

God is not going to hand out measly answers in response to big-time prayers. He loves it when we speak highly of him, and impossible prayers let him show off. Boldness in prayer demonstrates faith. It shows nothing is impossible with God. It's not that my faith has to match the big prayer. Instead, my faith in God's ability to do the impossible glorifies not me but my Father in heaven. God likes that kind of prayer because it can demonstrate to others how big he is. And whew! I'm off the hook with my less-than-mustard-seed-sized faith. But just a smidgen of faith in who God is and what he can do—why, that's enough.

How big are your prayers? Mountain-sized? We find another teaching on this relationship between faith and prayer in Mark 11:23–24, when Jesus explained faith-sized prayers:

> "I tell you the truth, if anyone says to this mountain, 'Go, throw yourself into the sea,' and does not doubt in his heart but believes that what he says will happen, it will be done for him. Therefore I tell you, whatever you ask for in prayer, believe that you have received it, and it will be yours."

What are your mountain-sized prayers about? A teenager who is sneaking out at night and skipping school the next day? A spouse who drowns out the day's stresses with a six-pack? The weight of guilt and shame from mistakes in your past? Jesus taught that whatever we ask for in prayer, we should believe that we have received it. That's also what he practiced: "Father, I thank you that you have heard me" (John 11:41). This is the prayer of thanksgiving—the faith prayer that is so sure of God's desire to do the impossible that the pray-er can thank God in advance of the answer.

Again, this doesn't mean that we ask God and thank him in advance for how he will make us millionaires. It's not a believe-it-receive-it formula. It's all about God and nothing about us.

It's about his ability, not ours. Pastor and writer Mark Batterson explains this well.

> Bold prayers honor God, and God honors bold prayers. God isn't offended by your biggest dreams or boldest prayers. He is offended by anything less. If your prayers aren't impossible to you, they are insulting to God. Why? Because they don't require divine intervention. But ask God to part the Red Sea or make the sun stand still or float an iron axhead, and God is moved to omnipotent action.[1]

God gets to be God—not only the one who can move mountains (have you ever felt an earthquake?), but the one who created them. I am continually reminded of his greatness as I look out the windows of my home in the Sierra Valley, the largest alpine valley in North America, where Italian-Swiss immigrants settled with their dairy cattle. And I've seen big answers to bold prayers for my community. I call this "praying beyond your reach."

In All Circumstances

Sometimes our prayers are puny, such as when we pray for a job—any job. When I lost my teaching position years ago, after the initial emotional shock, I challenged myself to thank God for what he was going to do. While one person close to me told me to send my résumé all over and see what came back, I knew in my heart of hearts that God was using the situation for something better. You see, I had been commuting across our mountain valley for many years to a larger community, and sensed that God would provide a more ideal position right in my little town instead. The summer went by and I heard nothing until the very last week before school started. A local school administrator called me and said that not one but *two* English teachers had just announced their retirement from the high school. Would I be interested in doing a long-term sub position and then applying for the permanent job?

Long story made short, I not only got the job, but God did his God Thing. My new salary schedule was significantly higher, and I collected unemployment compensation all summer, something teachers otherwise cannot do. My commute time went from sixty minutes to three minutes a day. And I would be teaching in the same town where my four children were. In fact, much to my oldest two children's dismay, I would be *their* English teacher. That was a good thing, despite their initial reaction. If I had not lost my job, I would have been under contract to another school district and would not have been free to take the new position. God knew the big, bold plan.

What if the big, bold prayer isn't answered? What if your marriage falls apart or your spouse dies from cancer or your child is killed? How do we thank God in the midst of such suffering? While I have certainly been through many challenges in my life, I have not faced those situations. But Carole Lewis, national director emeritus of First Place 4 Health, has. While her husband, Johnny, was dealing with Stage 4 cancer, a drunk driver killed their daughter Shari. She explains how thanksgiving prayer still played a part in her life:

> At the time of Shari's death, I never dreamed that thankfulness might be one of the things God would use to heal the huge void left in my heart. I know that people grieve in different ways and that everyone is different, but I have come to believe that being thankful *in the midst* of a tragic circumstance is the key to moving toward healing.[2]

Lewis went on to list seventeen situations related to her daughter's death for which she could give thanks, such as having the opportunity to travel with her one month prior to her death.

We cannot know all of God's purposes in allowing suffering in our lives. Lewis also writes, "As we thank Him for wherever we are right now, He comes through as our loving heavenly Father to soothe and heal our wounds."[3] In the midst of suffering we can thank our Father that he sent his Servant Son, who suffered on our behalf, so that we can know the loving provision of our heavenly Father. Jesus understands our suffering and intercedes on our behalf; the Father, who experienced loss when his Son died, hears our cries. We are never alone—and for that we can give thanks.

Thanksgiving prayer may be the most important kind, perhaps even more than praise. This comes from my perspective as a mom of four kids. When my kids would say, "You are such a great mom"—well, I appreciated that just fine. However, when they said, "Mom, thank you for all you did for me today" or "Thanks for hauling my friends and me around," I saw they noticed my investment in their lives and my love for them.

In any case, giving thanks to God the Father is important. When life is good and that answer comes, thanking God is a prayer of appreciation for what he has done. Thanking God in advance is that prayer of faith—it says, "I believe in you, Lord." We see from the Lazarus story that our thanksgiving prayers can build faith, and not just ours, but others' as well. And while Jesus taught that faith is required for prayer, faith is also the result of prayer. A thankful heart and prayer and faith are all interwoven—drawing us closer to the Father who wants us to live out our lives boldly.

PRAYER OF THANKSGIVING

Thank you, Lord, for being my strength and for protecting me. I will give you thanks forever. As I think about my past and how you have taken care of me, I see your faithfulness in each and every deed in my behalf. I am thankful for your faithful love toward me, and these are just some examples: When others tried to hurt me, you took care of me. When I was confused and cried out to you, you calmed me and showed me the right direction for me. When finances were looking bleak, you met each and every one of my needs. When I got myself into a mess, you helped me out of that dark situation and then redeemed the days of pain, even though I had created the situation myself. Your love for me never fails, and I thank you, Lord. I also know, Father, that I can thank you for what is ahead. Just like Jesus, I can thank you that you have heard me. I know you will continue to pour out your love on my family and me, because you are faithful, you hear me, and you answer your promises. In everything—including the challenges in my life—I give thanks. In Jesus' name, amen!

Adapted from Psalm 28:7; 30:12; 75:1; 100:4; 107:1–21;
John 11:41; 1 Thessalonians 5:18

GROWING IN *Prayer*

1. For what have you been thankful recently?

2. What do you think is the connection between prayers of praise and prayers of thanksgiving?

3. Review the story about Jesus' miracle of raising Lazarus in John 11. Why did Jesus pray the prayer he did (vv. 41–42)?

4. How are prayer and faith connected?

5. It is said that prayer can move mountains (see Mark 11:22–24). What miraculous answers to prayer have you witnessed?

6. How can we give thanks when life is hard?

7. For what are you thankful today?

Chapter 6

Jesus' Prayer in Trouble

You might think prayer doesn't happen on a public school campus, but believe me, it does. It may not be out loud and in-your-face obvious, but believing students pray, as do believing teachers. I needed wisdom and patience a lot as a teacher. And I prayed daily for my students—many of whom faced some of the most horrendous kinds of trouble and suffering you can imagine. Several students endured physical and emotional abuse at the hands of their parents. One student's father committed suicide in their home. Another student watched his best friend accidentally shoot himself in the head.

Teaching is the best—but perhaps also the hardest—profession. You invest your life into dozens or even hundreds of students five days a week, and often your heart aches for them as you watch them, counsel them, and try your best to support them through some of the toughest years of their lives. And sometimes they return the kindnesses to you when you are hurting as well. Thank goodness we serve a Savior who left us with a living example of how he prayed during the weeklong walk to the cross.

During the countdown to the cross, Jesus did not put on a happy face. Despite the fact that a throng had greeted him with "Hosanna!" and a carpet of palm branches, he knew they would fail him. While many were spreading the word about his raising Lazarus from the dead, he knew this would only propel the Pharisees to destroy him. Even the fact that a group of visiting Greeks had come for the Passover Feast in Jerusalem and wanted to meet Jesus seemingly did not puff him up. He was about his Father's mission—the salvation of those who would believe in him—and he was troubled.

Instead of performing more healings for the gathering crowd, he spoke of his imminent death:

> "The hour has come for the Son of Man to be glorified. I tell you the truth, unless a kernel of wheat falls to the ground and dies, it remains only a single seed. But if it dies, it produces many seeds. The man who loves his life will lose it, while the man who hates his life in this world will keep it for eternal life. Whoever serves me must follow me; and where I am, my servant also will be. My Father will honor the one who serves me.
>
> "Now my heart is troubled, and what shall I say? 'Father, save me from this hour'? No, it was for this very reason I came to this hour."
>
> John 12:23–27

And then we have Jesus' simple prayer in the next verse: "Father, glorify your name!" (John 12:28).

Wait a minute. That's how Jesus prays when he says his heart is troubled? After all, Jesus had just used such phrases as "the hour has come" and "if it dies" and "the man who loves his life will lose it." That kind of language not only is troubled in tone but also is indicative that the speaker is facing the end of his life. Nonetheless, his prayer is "Father, glorify your name!" We earlier looked at this passage from the context of listening prayer, because the Father is heard in response to Jesus' plea. This chapter, though, will focus on what we can learn from how Jesus prayed when the world was shaking him.

First, Jesus did not ask to be saved from trouble. Instead, he said, "What shall I say? 'Father, save me from this hour'?" (v. 27). That's a rhetorical question that he immediately answered, "No, it was for this very reason I came to this hour." Jesus knew that the earthly struggles that would lead to his death were part of his Father's plan. He did not pray that his Father remove them. He did not pray that the Father rescue him and whisk him away. He did not pray the prayer that most of us pray on at least a weekly basis: "Save me from this hour!"

So God Will Be Glorified

I administer my church's online prayer-warrior group. Weekly I take the requests that come via Sunday connection cards as well as those that come to me directly via our church's website and send them out to a team of fifty people who will pray. Most of those are for physical healing or for relief from some other kind of pain, such as struggles in a marriage or financial hardship. *Save me from this hour.* Wanting to be freed of physical suffering is a natural human instinct. After all, we pop pain relievers to get rid of the ordinary aches and pains. If *Save me from this hour* could be packaged and sold, it could make prayer lists a whole lot shorter each week.

But Jesus demonstrated that there is purpose in the trouble we face. If God allows it, God can use it in our lives. There has to be a reason for the "no" answer when the pain does not go away.

Jesus didn't escape trouble—he walked right into it. It was part of the plan for his life. Life on earth is not a happily-ever-after existence; even heroines in Disney movies struggle before they gain their prize. Does that mean, then, that we shouldn't pray *Save me from this hour*? After all, it's a basic human instinct to want to protect ourselves from harm. Jesus did teach us to pray boldly, so praying for the miracle is indeed just fine. But that's not the point of this prayer.

Notice how Jesus prays: "Father, glorify your name!" Our lives are meant to glorify God. In the good times, our lives—the way we react, our words, our actions, our attitudes—should bring honor to his name. The same is true of the harder times, too. The day before my dad died of complications relating to amyotrophic lateral sclerosis (Lou Gehrig's disease), he was having fun teasing his nurses. Dad was simply living out the last moments of his life as a Christian man would. Yes, it's very nice to see a Christian living the high life with every hair and accessory in place, but it's even more compelling when a suffering, dying Christian breathes life, love, and laughter into others until the very end. Jesus pointed the way to the Father. His prayer wasn't *Save me from this hour* but *Glorify your name!* His focus was always on the Father and his purpose for Jesus' life on earth.

This was a public prayer, as opposed to one up on a mountainside at night. Others were watching Jesus. He could have prayed for the Father to whisk him away, and that miracle could have been done. However, while the earlier miracles did bring attention and draw some others to faith, the greater purpose of Christ's walk on earth was that journey to the cross for the final provision of the salvation of mankind. The Father would indeed be glorified, as Christ prayed, because the ultimate sacrifice would change forever the way people would view the Creator—as the One True God who desired a relationship with his creation and valued each and every person enough to send his Son so others could know him and experience not only a life of meaning on earth but life everlasting with him.

The operative word in this short prayer for trouble seems to be *glorify*; it's a word that's not often used in conversational language today. We might hear, "I was a glorified secretary" or "That movie glorified violence," but we might not understand what we are saying when we pray that God "be glorified." The word *glorify* in the Greek is *doxazō*, which means to magnify, extol, or praise someone, especially God.[1] When we magnify God, we make him greater—which, if we think about it, is impossible, since he is unfathomably larger than any created thing. In that sense, though, we are holding him up for others to say, "Wow! God is great!" The attention all goes to God here in this prayerful attitude, instead of the self-focused *Save me from this hour* petition.

Greek scholar W. E. Vine explains that in this prayer Jesus was asking that God the Father reveal all that the Father is and all that he does. That glorification would be done through Christ, who was the earthly manifestation of God.[2] This isn't a *Make me look good* statement. Jesus was not puffed up by the attention of the palm wavers or the miracle seekers or the Greek inquirers. Jesus knew his mission was to point others to the way of life eternal, which would be faith in Christ as God's Son, the Messiah. God's glory would be brought to light as an act of God the Father through Jesus Christ.

So yes, we can pray, *Save me from this hour, Lord!* But if the trouble is not removed, we pray, *Father, glorify your name!* And in doing that, we can know that God will be glorified through us. This is a process of sanctification—a walk toward holiness. If we otherwise ask God to remove the trouble and struggle with resentment and bitterness, we are fighting the process of holiness. We are slowing down our own personal growth as Christians. And we may even be an embarrassment to those who bear his name and the church as a whole.

Meaning Out of Mess

In one of my years of teaching high school English, I had a particularly sassy young man who mocked me during class and made little effort to complete his work. When he was not happy with a low score on an assignment, I was not surprised when his mother requested a meeting. From the get-go she went into a loud rant with continual bad language, even though my administrator and another teacher were present. While I presented ample documentation to explain the assignment and his grade, she seemed bent on destroying me in front of the others. I remember thinking about just walking out of the room as she continued the long line of cuss words, and I know I prayed something like, *Save me from this hour*, but I sat there and took it, eventually asking God to somehow use me and receive honor out of the mess. That did not happen immediately. Both mother and son hated me for the rest of that year. However, when the sister became my student some years later, I prayed the same prayer: *Help me be Jesus to this family, Lord. Be manifested in me. Be glorified despite our history. Turn trouble into triumph.*

And that happened. The sister was one of my top students, got into several excellent colleges, and will graduate this year from a highly respected school. When I heard "Thank you for all you did" and "We couldn't have done it without your help" from mother and daughter at the end of that year, I simply hoped that God be glorified instead.

Our Father redeems our trouble when we pray, "Father, glorify your name!" A mess can become a way of salvation. Our trouble then makes perfect sense with its purposeful plan to raise up the name of our Lord. There is purpose in prayer beyond the simple result. Our Father in heaven is raised up. He is recognized for his rightful place as Creator and Lord of the universe. And part of the answer also lies in us—our sanctification, the process of holiness, so that this faithwalk works and so that others see that it works and make the choice to follow Jesus as well.

PRAYER IN TROUBLE

Lord, please be attentive to my cries, as trouble has fallen on me. Deliver me and protect me. Preserve my life, Father, and in your unfailing love, silence those who would do me harm. I know that I can call out to you when life gets hard. When I cast my cares on you, Father, you sustain me and keep me from falling. Even when I have brought trouble on myself because of my own sin, you have been patient with me and forgiven me. When fear overcomes me, you take hold of my hand, tell me not to be afraid, and help me. You are a hiding place for me, Lord, sheltering me from storms that would wash me to sea. I know you do not want me to worry about anything, so I lay my concerns at your feet and ask that your peace that passes understanding will guard my heart in Christ Jesus. Even though my heart is troubled right now, I ask that you be glorified in this situation and that my life will bring you honor. In Jesus' name, amen!

Adapted from Psalm 35:15,17; 143:10–11; 50:15; 55:22; 78:38–39; Isaiah 41:13; Nahum 1:7; Philippians 4:6–7

GROWING IN *Prayer*

1. What is it about trouble that sends people to prayer?
2. Review John 12:12–28. About what was Jesus troubled?
3. Why wouldn't Jesus pray to be saved from his trouble?

4. How could there be purpose in the struggles we face?

5. When Jesus prayed, "Father, glorify your name," how does this shift the focus related to the trouble?

6. What does it mean to glorify God?

7. What prayer needs do you have for anything that may be troubling you?

Chapter 7

Jesus' Prayer for Himself

The art of argumentation was one of the most important skills I taught to high school juniors and seniors in my English classes. Hopefully they learned how to recognize strategies writers and speakers use to create arguments, as well as how to create an effective argument themselves. Some even used what they had learned on me. Here's one example:

Student: "Mrs. McHenry, isn't the weather beautiful now after such a long, snowy winter?"

Teacher (who already knows where this is going): "Yes, I just love it."

Student: "Do you think we could work outside today? It's a shame that we have to stay cooped up in this classroom all day instead of outside enjoying the sun."

Teacher: "No, that usually doesn't go very well—too many distractions."

Student: "I had a feeling you'd say that, Mrs. McHenry, so I actually surveyed every student in the class ahead of time, and they all promised to get their work done."

Teacher: "That was very enterprising of you, but my research over the last twenty years only supports my argument that students get less work done when we go outside."

Student: "But prom is coming up, Mrs. McHenry, and we need to work on our tans. Besides, the principal said we could."

Teacher: "Johnny, you get an A in argumentation today by using all three appeals—to emotion, to logic, and to authority. I'm glad you've been listening in class, which is where we will continue to work today."

Jesus was a master of words, too. He used analogies and parables to make abstract ideas more understandable to the common people. He had to—as the people needed to understand that God in heaven had come to earth in the form of man, and his mission was to teach that eternal life could be grasped by faith in him. What if no one had believed? What if all the proof of his resurrection and deity were still plain as day—but no one would move out of their old religious prison to embrace the freedom of faith in Christ?

When people pray, they often make an argument with the Father, as we see in what is referred to as Jesus' priestly prayer in John 17. This occurred after he and the disciples had gathered in a large, furnished upper room, where the disciples prepared what we now call the Last Supper and where Jesus washed the disciples' feet. His prayer also followed several sad turns of events:

- A dispute among the disciples about who was the greatest (Luke 22:24).
- Jesus' statement that one would betray him—and then the quiet acknowledgment that it would be Judas Iscariot (Matthew 26:25).
- Continued confusion among the disciples about who Jesus really was (John 14:8).

- The prediction that Simon Peter would deny knowing Jesus three times (Luke 22:34).

After Jesus taught them the parable of the vine and the branches, warned them that the world would continue to hate them, and promised them that the Holy Spirit would come, he prayed the prayer that is the longest recorded prayer of his that we have. As it has three parts, each with a different focus, I have divided the prayer into those three parts for this chapter and the next two.

In the first part Jesus prays for himself:

> After Jesus said this, he looked toward heaven and prayed:
> "Father, the time has come. Glorify your Son, that your Son may glorify you. For you granted him authority over all people that he might give eternal life to all those you have given him. Now this is eternal life: that they may know you, the only true God, and Jesus Christ, whom you have sent. I have brought you glory on earth by completing the work you gave me to do. And now, Father, glorify me in your presence with the glory I had with you before the world began."
>
> John 17:1–5

Making His Case

There seem to be several parts to this section of Jesus' prayer: the resignation, the request, the rationale or argument, and a reiteration of the request.

Our Master Teacher seems to be making an argument with this priestly prayer. While the Lord's Prayer was short and to the point, this John 17 prayer uses reasoning and explanation. Every rhetor or orator knows his or her audience and how to appeal to that particular group. As with every other prayer, Jesus addresses God as "Father"—not only his "nourisher, protector, upholder,"[1] but also his biological parent. This is the same Father to whom he prayed, "I thank you that you have heard me" (John 11:41), and from whom he heard, "This is my Son, whom I love. . . . Listen to him!" (Matthew 17:5). As an audience, the Father listened and cared—and answered Jesus, meeting his each and every need. Jesus used the term *Father* 189 times.[2] You also can call God *Father*. And you can expect the same response as you take your petitions to the Father "because he cares for you" (1 Peter 5:7).

The Resignation

The first sentence is a resignation: "Father, the time has come" (John 17:1). In argumentation this statement could be said to create a sense of immediacy or urgency. It's similar to saying, "Voting day is tomorrow, so you need to make up your mind today." It's a reverse of what Jesus said at the wedding at Cana when he told his mother, Mary, "My time has not yet come" (John 2:4). Mary was nudging him into ministry at that time, when instead Jesus knew there was a finite, fixed and calendared plan for his walk toward the cross.

Can we also pray, *God, I'm in a bind—please answer me today?* If we are honest in our prayers, we do. The various psalmists did.

- "Do not be far from me, for trouble is near and there is no one to help." (Psalm 22:11)
- "But I cry to you for help, O Lord; in the morning my prayer comes before you." (Psalm 88:13)
- "Out of the depths I cry to you, O Lord; O Lord, hear my voice." (Psalm 130:1–2)

We can pray, *Father, the time has come. This is my Waterloo. It's the great test. I need you. Please show up.* Does such a prayer get any more attention than something less desperate, more distanced, less emotional? Does a mother turn her ears more quickly toward her child if he cries out in need? While I certainly did, I recognize that I am human, and God is God. But I do believe he hears our heart cries as we resign ourselves to the tough circumstances we face.

The Request

In this prayer Jesus makes the same request as the prayer in the last chapter: "Glorify your Son, that your Son may glorify you." Again, Jesus asks to be glorified so that he will glorify the Father in what is ahead for him. In everything Jesus is about to do, he wants to honor God. His disciples will fail him. They will fall asleep when he asks them to stand watch and pray for him. One will betray him—turn him over to Roman authorities, who will arrest him. Another follower will deny him several times. Then there will be the trial, the beatings, and the cross. Nonetheless, Jesus' greatest desire is that God's light shine through him. He does not want to receive the honor—but only wants his life to be a mirror that reflects others' praise to his Father in heaven. He wants them to be directed to eternal salvation through a relationship with God in heaven.

The Rationale

To his audience, the Father, Jesus presents his argument. It's not a request to save him from pain or trouble or heartache. It's a simple request that within the struggles ahead, Jesus be glorified so others are redirected heavenward. It's a *Use me for your sake, Father* prayer. When we are passionately pursuing God's will for our lives, we do not need pats on the back—we have the Father's nod of approval instead. We do not need to splash our well-cooked feast on social media in pursuit of hundreds of Likes. Knowing that others see Jesus in us should be enough reward.

Jesus supports his request with reasoning: a rationale that starts with the word *for*, or in other words, *because*. And here's the *because*, as Jesus makes his case. First, the Father himself gave Jesus authority over all people (v. 2). Second, he did this so others would have eternal life (v. 2). The authority given Jesus is not for his glory but for others' benefit of a relationship with the Father. Then Jesus defines *eternal life* (v. 3), another good strategy in argumentation—not that God needs a term defined, but we should remember that the disciples were listening in, too, and they were still at least 50 percent clueless about why Jesus had come, and had even less understanding of why he had to die. Jesus said, "Now this is eternal life: that they may know you, the only true God, and Jesus Christ, whom you have sent." Ah, third, he gives the gospel message right there. Rules do not lead to eternal life—the relationship with the only true God does. And this relationship comes via the God-sent Jesus Christ. The purpose of this prayer is to ask the Father that Jesus' life lead others to eternity.

This is a sure-fire prayer request for our Note-to-Self edification. If we want guarantees on how to throw up prayer requests that stick, we can pray that whatever we ask, it only be for the purpose of others coming to know the Father. No tongue-in-cheek request for the moon so I'll shine like Jesus . . . and coincidentally hit the bestsellers list. No—just for the saving of souls, not my savings account.

In argumentation the reason alone is not sufficient. You also need specific support for the reasoning. This is done through an example, an analogy, statistics, or other appeal to logos—in other words, logic. To high school students I taught that *logos* was a Greek word that meant "logic." A logos appeal is one that appeals to our brain, our thinking, those reasoning skills formed by use of inductive reasoning, deductive reasoning, or cause-and-effect reasoning.

However, it's interesting that the first dictionary definition for the word *Logos* is "the divine wisdom manifest in the creation, government, and redemption of the world and often identified with the second person of the Trinity."[3] Jesus, who was the Word in the beginning and who is the Word made flesh. When we use our best reasoning, we are one in thinking with the Word. And in his prayer Jesus uses himself to support his argument and to lend authority (yet another form of argumentative appeal) to that argument. He prays, "I have brought you glory on earth by completing the work you gave me to do." Jesus asked for the Father to glorify him, so that any praise would point others toward the Father. And he supports his request by offering evidence—Jesus had completed his earthly mission and was redirecting others toward the Father. Picture one of those kids in a sandwich costume at an intersection, waving a giant arrow—not to around the corner but toward heaven. That's what Jesus did: "Hey, look at me, but only so I can show you this great deal TODAY in heaven!"

That brings us to an assumed warrant of this prayer. In argumentation a warrant is an assumption the speaker could make of the audience. Here Jesus must assume that the Father wants to be glorified and wants all people to know him. Again, these warrants serve to cement the prayer deal for Jesus.

Reiteration of Request

Good speakers make sure their listeners understand the argument, so often there is a reiteration of the argument at the end of the speech—a call to action for the audience. Jesus does this in verse 5 of his priestly prayer in John 17: "And now, Father, glorify me in your presence with the glory I had with you before the world began." Two other kinds of appeals occur again in this part of the prayer. He makes an emotional appeal by calling God "Father," and he makes an appeal to authority by mentioning his position as part of the triune God. All in all, this short prayer makes a solid argument, one that we know is fulfilled with Christ's crucifixion and resurrection. Jesus did return to his Father in heaven, and both continue to be glorified today—by the natural world, by people on earth, and certainly by heavenly beings.

In My Life, Lord . . .

We have much to take away from Jesus' prayer for himself. As we pray, we need to face facts—understand what is true about our situation and deal with what currently exists. We can't wish it away. What would that sound like? Maybe this: *Lord, the time has come. The place has come. The situation has come. And here I have come for the purpose of glorifying you. May others see you through me.*

When we pray, we can also simply state what we want—as did Jesus—but frame that within the context of our desire to bring people closer to God. In our college days at Christian gatherings, Craig and I sang a chorus, "In My Life, Lord, Be Glorified." As we are honest and earnest while praying those words, it would be hard to pray anything that would not make the Father smile with approval.

Do we need reasoning in our prayers? A rationale? Would God not know our reasons, our intent, the background information, the clever analogy, the modern-day parable? None of that is needed, is it? After all, that's what Jesus was demonstrating with the Lord's Prayer. Keep it simple, right? And clearly, God knows all that. Author and speaker Jennifer Kennedy Dean writes,

> You don't need to build a theological case for why God should want to meet your need. He wants to meet your need because He's your daddy and you are the apple of His eye. Jesus highlights the simplicity of supplication by saying, "Ask and it will be given you. . . . For everyone who asks receives" (Matthew 7:7–8).[4]

For what purpose, then, would someone throw in all that filler? The reason is you.

God wants you to agree with him. That is part of the purpose of prayer. And when we are so self-absorbed, thinking about our needs and our worries and our words and our schedule even, we aren't really praying, are we? The famous nineteenth-century preacher Charles Spurgeon put this well when he wrote,

> Let us remember that the main point of supplication is not to pray in the presence of others or in your own presence but to present your prayer before God. It is clear that this means that the prayer is to be directed to God. That sounds so simple, and yet how often we forget it. Like a playful child, we get our bow and arrows and shoot them anywhere.[5]

Forgive me if I make warrants (assumptions) about you. I'll speak of myself here. On any given Sunday in church it is thoroughly my intent to worship the Lord with all my heart, soul, mind, and strength. But as I'm standing there in the eleventh pew, left-hand side, singing the first, second, and perhaps even third song, I realize my thoughts have bounced from three conversations with friends, to the grocery list, and finally to where we might have lunch afterward. *Wow. Hello, God, this is supposed to be for you.* And then I focus in and offer the last verse up to the Father with a hope that his grace will again cover my self-focus.

My point is that as we pray, perhaps the words we utter or think may not necessarily be ones we'd like to see in print. Perhaps they're not prayers at all if I am so wrapped up in a blanket of self-sympathy. Perhaps it takes some elaboration with examples or rationale until we truly have shed the distractions that keep us from actual prayer, which brings us into communion and union with the Father we say we love.

94

Here's a question: How would the answered prayer change you? Would you be closer to the Father if he said yes? Would there be less of self that others would see and more of him in you? Would the Father be glorified through the end result? While prayer can be analyzed in terms of argumentation, it's not an exact science, and it's certainly not an art of manipulation. Instead, prayer is an opportunity for each of us to become more like Christ as we choose that the heart of God be made manifest in our lives. *In my life, my work, my family, my church, my song, be glorified today, Lord.*

PRAYER FOR OURSELVES

Lord, I ask that you be glorified through me, but I well know that I have fallen short and that only through your grace am I acceptable in your sight. While it is only logical that I ask for your favor in my life, instead, Father, I ask that you make me more like you, so that I see your hand in each and every day of my life—whether those days are lovely or pain-filled. Keep your words in my heart so that my life is rich with your presence. I pray that you will write love and faithfulness on the tablet of my heart, so as to win favor and a good name in your sight as well as that of others, only so that they draw near to you. I will trust you with all my heart and will lean not on my own understanding. In all my ways I pray I will acknowledge your hand in my life, so that you make my paths straight. Give me your wisdom so that I make good choices for my personal health and well-being. I will choose to honor you with any wealth you choose to give me and will be generous with my tithe and with other charitable giving. Father God, I will accept any discipline you have for me, as I know you would allow it for my good. Above all else, I ask that you be glorified through me, so others are drawn to you. In Jesus' name, amen.

Adapted from John 17:1–5; Romans 3:23; Proverbs 3:1–12

GROWING IN *Prayer*

1. Do you find that you present an argument to God when you pray? If not, why not? If you do, can you think of an example?

2. Read John 17:1–5 and put this prayer in your own words.

3. When Jesus prayed, "The time has come," what do you think he meant?

4. What reason does Jesus give for his request that the Father glorify him?

5. If God's plan was already in motion, why do you think Jesus prayed this prayer?

6. How could our prayers be less focused on self and more on the God we serve?

7. What deep need for prayer do you have right now? Write that down or share it with your small group.

Chapter 8

Jesus' Prayer for Friends

How can I help you?" was my go-to question as I monitored my classes. If I had said, "Do you need help?" the answer usually would have been *no*. I figured that even my best students had a need, and even if they were already doing A-level work, they could still learn something and improve. Our Master Teacher also helped out his disciples—with prayer.

The longest of the three sections of the Upper Room prayer in John 17 is his intercession for his friends, the disciples—his co-workers who would become responsible for spreading the gospel message. In the first section Jesus introduces the subject and his reason for bringing the matter to prayer:

> "I have revealed you to those whom you gave me out of the world. They were yours; you gave them to me and they have obeyed your word. Now they know that everything you have given me comes from you. For I gave them the words you gave me and they accepted them. They knew with certainty that I came from you, and they believed that you sent me. I pray for them. I am not praying for the world, but for those you have

given me, for they are yours. All I have is yours, and all you have is mine. And glory has come to me through them. I will remain in the world no longer, but they are still in the world, and I am coming to you."

John 17:6–11

A great responsibility weighed on Jesus' shoulders. His Father gave him the twelve disciples for the purpose of revealing the plan of salvation: faith in Jesus Christ, the Son of God, sent by the Father. Jesus acknowledged several things in this part of the prayer:

God gave him the disciples.

Jesus revealed himself to them.

The disciples believed that Jesus had come from the Father.

The disciples obeyed God's word.

The disciples came out of the world—from the fishing nets and the tax collector's booth and zealous politics—to follow an unknown carpenter for three years in towns around the Sea of Galilee and beyond. Jesus would die on the cross the very next day after this prayer. What would become of the twelve men who had left their life's work for the work of God? Jesus knew there was a plan, but he also knew life for these men who had given up everything for him would not be easy. He loved these men and told the Father, "They are yours." He had been the teacher, mentor, and guide, but he would be leaving and needed the Father's assurance that the disciples would have the care they would need.

When I retired from teaching, I learned that my high school juniors were upset I was leaving; they were feeling abandoned and hurt. I actually scheduled a meeting with the whole junior class one day the last week of school to tell them I loved them and that I was not leaving them because I didn't like them, but that it simply was time for me to go. I also said that I had chosen that particular time to retire because I had full confidence in their academic strength and leadership qualities as a class to carry into their final year of school. I left pages and pages of month-by-month instructions for the people who would take over my duties, particularly as senior-class adviser and academic adviser. In other words, I wanted to make sure my students were going to be more than just okay: I wanted to make sure they would fly. And actually they are. The day I wrote this chapter was their graduation day; all of those young people have excellent plans for the future, and almost all of them are going to college. Jesus wanted to ensure a bright future for his disciples, too.

The Handoff

In the beginning of the prayer, Jesus again acknowledged that his work with the disciples was done. He offered himself and the disciples up to the Father. It was a handoff—a passing of the baton—from Son to Father. This is a prayer teachers and parents offer up a lot: *Here they are, Lord. I've finished the work with them; now they're yours.* It's not an I-don't-know-what-to-do-with-them prayer. Jesus did indeed know what to do as he taught and modeled a new way of living out faith and loving others by serving them. He had been entrusted with the disciples by the Father until that moment; now he was entrusting the Father with the rest of their lives.

Likewise, we give our best offering to our friends and family and co-workers. We live out our calling in the best way we know how, according to the guidance we get through God's Word and through his nudges in prayer, in circumstances, and through others. At some point, though, a good parent, friend, or boss may not be able to provide for or fix the needs others have. Then we pray. We offer up those in need as Jesus did. *Lord, I've done what you have called me to do with this person you have brought into my life. I give him to you now for your care.* It's not easy, the offering part of prayer. But going to our good, good Father on that person's behalf is the best thing we can do.

Jesus has four focuses of prayer for the disciples, which we find in the rest of the prayer:

> "Holy Father, protect them by the power of your name—the name you gave me—so that they may be one as we are one. While I was with them, I protected them and kept them safe by that name you gave me. None has been lost except the one doomed to destruction so that Scripture would be fulfilled.
>
> "I am coming to you now, but I say these things while I am still in the world, so that they may have the full measure of my joy within them. I have given them your word and the world has hated them, for they are not of the world any more than I am of the world. My prayer is not that you take them out of the world but that you protect them from the evil one. They are not of the world, even as I am not of it. Sanctify them by the truth; your word is truth. As you sent me into the world, I have sent them into the world. For them I sanctify myself, that they too may be truly sanctified."
>
> John 17:11–19

Our Master Teacher's four requests are for protection for the disciples, for their unity, for the joy of Christ within them, and for their sanctification.

Protection by the Power of His Name

The first request is "Holy Father, protect them by the power of your name—the name you gave me" (John 17:11). This is the only time Jesus uses the name *Holy Father*, a mix of the reverential with the familiar, the "remoteness with the nearness."[1] Later in the prayer Jesus reiterated this by asking that the Father not take the disciples out of the world but protect them from the evil one (John 17:15). He knew his Father would always be with the disciples, but he also knew that danger was imminent. Boldness would be required for the gospel mission after his death, and boldness would invite the Jewish and Roman authorities to wipe out the vestiges left after the crucifixion.

Many times while Jesus ministered, he chose to withdraw or chose not to enter a certain town because opposition was organizing against him. Once he left the earth, he would not be there to whisk away the disciples from potential disasters. While Jesus' work was done, the disciples' work was just starting. They would face hate, jealousy, injustice, and cruelty. They would face snares of the enemy, who would be raging after the resurrection. Tradition holds that each of the twelve disciples (Matthias replaced Judas Iscariot) died for his faith, except perhaps John, who was exiled. Twice Jesus asked for protection in this prayer—the first by the power of "your name—the name you gave me."

The name of *Jesus* or *Jesus Christ* has power in prayer. He himself taught his disciples to use it, in three instances in John's gospel in the Upper Room following the Last Supper:

- "And I will do whatever you ask in my name, so that the Son may bring glory to the Father. You may ask me for anything in my name, and I will do it" (John 14:13–14).
- "You did not choose me, but I chose you and appointed you to go and bear fruit—fruit that will last. Then the Father will give you whatever you ask in my name" (John 15:16).
- "In that day you will no longer ask me anything. I tell you the truth, my Father will give you whatever you ask in

my name. Until now you have not asked for anything in my name. Ask and you will receive, and your joy will be complete" (John 16:23–24).

We have a privileged position in prayer in that we know Jesus Christ as personal Savior and Lord. Jesus taught that when we claim that privileged position by using his name, he and the Father will do what we ask and that our joy will be complete.

Privilege is not to be taken lightly. We know this from personal experience. We might apply for a job at a friend's place of employment using his name and, because he is well respected, we might get the job. That does not mean, however, that our résumé is lacking; it only means that our background, education, and skills are more readily recognized because of our connection. Similarly, the prayer request still must align with God's character and his plan for our own or others' lives. Herbert Lockyer, a classic writer on the subject of prayer, wrote, "The prime motive at the back of all our praying should be the glory of God."[2] We see this in Jesus' statement in John 14:13, "so that the Son may bring glory to the Father." The end result of the prayer should be that God is glorified. Lockyer writes that this is the "supreme prayer secret" and is the highest purpose we must aspire to in all our prayers. Our prayer objective is to be in unison with Christ's as we pray in his name.[3]

Unity Like That of Father and Son

The second request Jesus makes is that the disciples be unified: "That they may be one as we are one." Jesus had earlier told them, "I and the Father are one" (John 10:30), and he wanted the same kind of oneness of mind, heart, and soul for the disciples. In fact, unity would be essential for the disciples after his death, as it would be for the new church. This is certainly still true today.

Without unity the church is seen as petty, judgmental, and unloving. When Christians are mean-spirited and factious, others are repelled rather than drawn in. When churches split, neither side wins, friends and families are divided, and nonbelievers view the whole situation as a mess. And who wants to visit a mess?

When I first attended my church in Reno, Nevada, I attended a ministries fair, looking from table to table for the prayer ministry. When I asked the pastor's wife where I would find it, she said, "We don't have a prayer ministry. Would you start one?" So I did. One of the prayer ministries we now have at The Bridge Church is the prayer team, for which a handful of us meet one hour before church to pray for its leadership. After we pray with the pastor, we pray over the worship area, and one request I have each week is that we would be one as Jesus and the Father are one. Praying reader, this prayer for unity is essential. But note that the hinge of the prayer moves importantly on Jesus' statement that he and the Father are one. We don't want a church that blindly rubber-stamps anything and everything that comes down the pastoral pike. We want our leaders to be one with the Lord and the Father, so that they indeed are one with each other. Oneness occurs when each of us has the mindset and heart focus of the Almighty.

The Full Measure of Jesus' Joy

The third request of Jesus was that the disciples would have his joy within them—the *full* measure of his joy. The Greek word for joy here, *xapá* (*chara*) connotes the sense or awareness of God's grace—or "grace recognized."[4] Even in a tornado of tough circumstances, if we recognize that God's grace is our gravity force keeping us standing and focused on God's sovereign purpose, we can experience joy. Jesus did not merely want the disciples to survive the rest of their earthly days; he wanted them to thrive with testimonies that would cause others to take notice. He wanted those nonbelievers to scratch their heads and beg the answers to these questions: What brings you such peace and joy? How does your faith sustain you? Who is this Jesus Christ whom you believe? And what can I do to have the same joy you do?

Jesus prayed that the disciples would have the *full* measure of *his* joy within them. Yet he was facing not only death but also separation from his Father, so how on earth could he have been joy-filled? His earthly circumstances could not have provided joy. His own community—Nazareth—and even his family had no honor for him. While crowds followed him, most were looking for a healing touch—not necessarily for a Savior to follow. And the Jewish and Roman authorities were closing in on him. Jesus knew joy was not found in circumstances but in doing his Father's work. We see that as Jesus continues the prayer: "I have given them your word and the world has hated them, for they are not of the world any more than I am of the world." When God plants his word inside of us, joy is found when we hear that call on our lives and obey him. Personally, I found that even though teaching was exhaustingly hard, I could still find joy in my work because I knew I was following the Father's call on my life. The Master Teacher had called me to teach, serve, and love students, and no circumstances ever snuffed out the light of that call on my life. Just as Jesus prayed for joy for his disciples, we can pray for joy for those who work or serve with us as they live out the call on their lives.

Sanctification by the Truth of the Word

Jesus' last request of the Father for the disciples was that they would be sanctified by the truth of God's Word. He added, "As you sent me into the world, I have sent them into the world. For them I sanctify myself, that they too may be truly sanctified"

(John 17:18–19). Because the disciples were pulled out of the world to follow Jesus, they were no longer of it, Jesus said. They were following Jesus, not the rites of the Jewish faith, not the whims of their families, and not the laws of the Roman Empire. Their following Jesus had made them different, but they were still in a growth process. Unfortunately, sanctification isn't a magic wand; it requires each believer to pursue the separation from evil things and ways in a faithful manner. It cannot be transferred from one person to another but is built up, little by little, as a result of obeying God's Word and following the example of Christ in the power of the Holy Spirit.[5] There is a tandem relationship between the Word and the Truth: Jesus is the Word, and Jesus is the Truth. As we believe and embrace the Word, the Truth brings about sanctification in us. While some may think that sanctification is following a set of beliefs or rules, the opposite is true: The holiness process of sanctification brings about freedom—freedom from the chains of sin and freedom from condemnation. We pray that our friends, family, co-workers, and we will become more like Christ so we all can experience the freedom to live a life that is whole and purposeful.

There are a couple of other instances in the gospels when Jesus mentioned praying for his disciples. The first was recorded in Luke 22:31–32 after the Lord's Supper, when some of the disciples had the conversation about who would be the greatest, and Jesus told Peter that he would deny Jesus three times before the rooster crowed. He said, "Simon, Simon, Satan has asked to sift you as wheat. But I have prayed for you, Simon, that your faith may not fail. And when you have turned back, strengthen your brothers." Jesus knew Peter would cave under the threat of punishment or death and deny that he knew him, so Jesus prayed that Peter's faith would not fail . . . completely. Peter would be a key player in the spreading of the Christian faith; Jesus needed him to hang tough.

The other instance is referenced in Luke 10:2 but more thoroughly in Matthew 9:36–38:

> When he saw the crowds, he had compassion on them, because they were harassed and helpless, like sheep without a shepherd. Then he said to his disciples, "The harvest is plentiful but the workers are few. Ask the Lord of the harvest, therefore, to send out workers into his harvest field."

Here is yet another implication that Jesus was concerned that the good news might not reach every corner. This is still a needed prayer today. Wycliffe Bible Translators reports that as of this writing, a Bible translation exists for 3,223 languages in the world. However, even though there are 2,422 translation projects around the world in process now, there are still an estimated 1,700 to 1,800 languages that need Bible translation. Praying for workers for the harvest is still a need.

In Jesus' prayer for his disciples, we see his love and concern for the disciples as well as his desire that his Father be glorified through them. When we have compassion for those around us—our family, our friends, our co-workers, our neighbors—at the center of those prayers will be a desire for their protection, unity, joy, sanctification, and faithfulness. As God answers those prayers of ours, there will be plentiful workers for his harvest.

PRAYER FOR OTHERS

Lord God, you have put many special people in my life: my family, friends, people with whom I work, neighbors, and those in ministry. I am thankful for each one of them. I pray that I am a faithful example to them—that I am living out your Word in my life by pursuing my relationship with you and through what I do and say. I ask that they come to a personal relationship with you through your Son, Jesus Christ, and that they grow in faith. After all, Lord, they are yours. Holy Father, protect them by the power of your name and Jesus Christ. Keep them safe from the influence of the enemy and from all other harm. I also ask that we all be of one heart, mind, and soul as we pursue life together—just as you and your Son are one. Even through the struggles of this earth, Father, grant them the joy found only in Jesus and a peace that passes understanding. And above all, Lord, I ask that you sanctify them—nudge them along the path you have placed before them, helping them to choose holiness over temptation, justice over evil, and compassion over criticism. All of this I only ask so that you and your Son, Jesus, are glorified, so that the gospel of salvation is made manifest through our lives. In Jesus' name, amen!

Adapted from John 17:6–19; Philippians 4:7

GROWING IN *Prayer*

1. What kinds of prayers do you typically pray for your friends and family?

2. For whom does Jesus pray in John 17:6–19?

3. Why did Jesus remember them in prayer?

4. What were four different requests that Jesus made for the disciples?

5. Which of them resonates most personally for you? Is there any one that seems more important than another?

6. What does Jesus teach that gives particular power to our prayers? Why is that so?

7. What person's needs are especially weighing on your heart today? Spend some time praying for that person.

Chapter 9

Jesus' Prayer for the Church

M any years ago our school had a problem. Our teaching staff of only a dozen needed a new teacher who could teach both art and beginning algebra. How could such a person exist, with both right-brained and left-brained thinking and teaching abilities? This is a common issue for rural schools—requiring faculty to teach across curricular areas. As soon as I heard of our need for such a person, I turned to my Master Teacher and I began praying.

It just so happened that Laura was looking for a midlife change. She had been working at the corporate level in insurance in the San Francisco Bay Area, but she wanted to do something more purposeful with her college background in art. As I found out later, she was also a believer and paid attention to the Master Teacher's nudges. In fact, one day she felt led to drive into our alpine valley, where she read a local advertisement for the teaching position. For some reason, it seemed to be a personal invitation, and as she thought about it, she loved the idea of a complete life change.

The first day I met Laura after our school district hired her, our faculty met for lunch at a local restaurant. As I drove her there, I told her I had prayed for her. "And here you are!" I said, blinking back tears.

She smiled, also obviously emotional. "And because you prayed, here I am."

You, reader, are here today reading this book because people have prayed for you. Among those might be a grandmother or a friend or someone with whom you work. However, one of those people is a given: Jesus.

In the last section of the Upper Room prayer, Jesus not only prayed for his disciples, but also for *future* believers:

"My prayer is not for them alone. I pray also for those who will believe in me through their message, that all of them may be one, Father, just as you are in me and I am in you. May they also be in us so that the world may believe that you have sent me. I have given them the glory that you gave me, that they may be one as we are one; I in them and you in me. May they be brought to complete unity to let the world know that you sent me and have loved them even as you have loved me.

"Father, I want those you have given me to be with me where I am, and to see my glory, the glory you have given me because you loved me before the creation of the world.

"Righteous Father, though the world does not know you, I know you, and they know that you have sent me. I have made you known to them, and will continue to make you known in order that the love you have for me may be in them and that I myself may be in them."

John 17:20–26

Grasp the significance of this: Jesus prayed this prayer for you. Moments after he prayed for you, he crossed the Kidron River and walked into the Garden of Gethsemane, where he was arrested. You were on his mind and heart just before he would knowingly walk into the trap of betrayal, so that he could give his life for your sake.

I don't know how you may be reacting to this, but I find that all of Jesus' biography and prayer theology gets very personal with this prayer. This is where I begin to insert "Janet" into his words to his Father. *My prayer is not for the disciples alone. I also pray for Janet, who will believe in me through my disciples' message, that Janet and other believers may be one, Father, just as you are in me and I am in you.* I feel it's as though I'm hearing my name mentioned in a whispered conversation at a party. I turn more intently toward the page. What, Jesus? Me? And what would you pray on my behalf, Lord?

Unity of the Church

The first of Jesus' requests is for unity—not just for the disciples but also for all who will believe because of the disciples' work to spread the gospel message. He asks that you and I, as well as the rest of the *all*, will be one—as Jesus and the Father are one. Unity, so others see us and believe in Jesus. That's a heavy responsibility. In other words, we need to be different from the rest of the crowd. We need to be loving. We need to stop bickering about politics and church matters and family differences. We need to care for one another. This unity of believers is essential so that outsiders are drawn to the faith, not repelled by the behavior of those who say they believe. Simply put, do our actions draw people to Jesus or repel them?

The worst in people often comes out in parent-teacher conferences. Unfortunately, one of the most dreaded of those conferences at my school was with a woman who wore "Jesus is my rock" T-shirts. She would enter the room with search-and-destroy words aimed at the teacher. While I never taught her student, my friend, who is not a Christian, did, and suffered from the woman's blame game, which was never pointed toward the student. More than once my friend said, "And I thought she was supposed to be a Christian."

A love that breeds unity is a subtle form of evangelism. It's infectious in the most wonderful way. People are drawn to others when they see love in the room, because it is also accompanied with patience, kindness, thoughtfulness, grace, and hope. Unity overlooks the faults of others who may not yet be living up to their potential, because unity knows those folks are growing in the right direction. Unity keeps confidences and does not listen to mean-spirited remarks. When others see unity, they say, "I want to be a part of that group. Where do I sign on?"

Unity is connected to the mission of Jesus, who came to unite those who would believe in an everlasting relationship with the Father.[1] Understanding God's love for us and embracing that love draws us together, believer to believer. In fact, if we say we want to grow closer to Christ, promoting and living out unity in our local church will need to be part of that process. After all, the standard for unity is the Father-Son relationship, and our union leads to communion—with God and his Son—"a communion of love displayed in a setting of glory."[2] When we bicker and nitpick and backbite, the world will not know that we are emissaries from God, and it will not see his glory in us or know his love.

A Future in His Presence

A second request of Jesus in this prayer is that future believers would be with Jesus so as to see the glory his Father lovingly gave him before the world was created. In stating this, Jesus said, "I want . . ." The meaning of this particular language means not "I'd like" but "I will that."[3] This has the same effect as a last will and testament. This is how he wanted his estate to be passed on—he wanted us to be with him. The best gift he could leave for future believers was eternal presence with him. Just as the Father loved the Son before he created the world, Jesus loved us before we were born. This gift makes sense, as earlier Jesus had said, "I came that they may have life and have it abundantly" (John 10:10 ESV).

If I could will something to my former students, it would be a personal relationship with Jesus Christ, which I found as a college sophomore. One night one of my roommates, Linda, and a neighbor, Bill, invited me to a free movie. College students love freebies—and I was no exception. The title character of the film, *For Pete's Sake,* produced by the Billy Graham Evangelistic Association, learns for the first time that he can have a personal relationship with Christ. While I had attended church my whole life, I had never heard that you can have a *personal* relationship with God—and that word—*personal*— echoed in my head until the film's end, when I stood to make a commitment to invite Jesus into my heart and follow him. That free film introduced me to the free gift of eternal life, which I accepted simply by standing and saying that prayer. The greatest joy, then, in my teaching career has not been learning of a student's great SAT scores or of her acceptance into a wonderful college, but hearing from her in an email or a message that she made a personal commitment to Christ. The best prayer we can pray may be that the ones we love will find Christ and follow him for the rest of their lives.

The Go-Between

The last of the three requests Jesus made was more of a declaration that he himself intended to carry out. He prayed that the love the Father has for him would be in those who know him and that he himself would be in them. Jesus lived so others would believe. His mission was for people to believe in the love of God as seen through the Son's sacrifice. Imparting the knowledge of God through Christ was the act of imparting love, because God is love. "Christ knew the reality and power of the love of the Father for him and asked that this might brighten and warm the lives of those who were his, with whom his life was now so closely bound up."[4] This was no *Save me* prayer, as Jesus immediately afterward purposefully walked into the place of ambush.

When we pray for people, we call this intercession, which derives from the Latin words *inter*, which means "between," and *cedere*, which means "go."[5] In other words, we are a go-between from a person in need right to the Lord God Almighty—just as Jesus was a go-between from heaven to men on earth. We love in prayer, just as Jesus loved prayerfully and prayed lovingly. Our hearts spilled out in prayer—that is intercession.

Charles Spurgeon once preached a sermon on this subject, concluding the following:

Then, again, permit me to say, how are you to prove your love to Christ or to his church if you refuse to pray for men? "We know that we have passed from death unto life, because we love the brethren." If we do not love the brethren, we are still dead. I will aver no man loves the brethren who does not pray for them. What! It is the very least thing you can do, and if you do not perform the least, you certainly will fail in the greater. You do not love the brethren unless you pray for them. . . . Let me ask you again how is it that you hope to get your own prayers answered if you never plead for others? Will not the Lord say, "Selfish wretch, thou art always knocking at my door, but it is always to cry for thine own welfare and never for another's; inasmuch as thou hast never asked for a blessing for one of the least of these my brethren, neither will I give a blessing to thee. Thou lovest not the saints, thou lovest not thy fellow men, how canst thou love me whom thou hast not seen, and how shall I love thee and give thee the blessing which thou askest at my hands?" Brethren, again I say I would earnestly exhort you to intercede for others, for how can you be Christians if you do not? Christians are priests, but how priests if they offer no sacrifice? Christians are lights, but how lights unless they shine for others? Christians are sent into the world, even as Christ was sent into the world, but how sent unless they are sent to pray? Christians are meant not only to be blessed themselves, but in them shall all the nations of the earth be blessed, but how if you refuse to pray?[6]

Our intercession for others is a practical demonstration of the love we say we have. This may be the Father's favorite form of prayer, our hearts laid out there in real-world moments and minutes and hours on behalf of someone else—Jesus in us loving others so much that we serve as the go-between from earth to heaven. An earthly advocate for a heavenly response.

Every year as a high school teacher I was asked to advocate for students in the form of recommendation letters. Each one took a good hour or more to write, as I did my best to present that young person in his or her best possible light. I'd speak of their strongest personal qualities, supported by their many academic and athletic accomplishments, as well as their volunteer and work experience. To some extent, with each letter I wrote I was staking my reputation on that kid. If he or she didn't live up to my guarantee that the organization would be honored through that student's studies, I would look bad. In fact, the organization might not believe the next letter I wrote if the student failed to do well. I wasn't prone to exaggeration—I would not write anything that was not true—but I knew well, for example, that Mr. X had forgotten an assignment or two and that Miss Y tended to be tardy. But because I had learned the importance of advocacy when I worked in my husband's law office for ten years, I knew it was my job to extend grace for the past as I championed each young person in my letters. Advocacy is a tricky business. And intercessory prayer is advocacy.

That's what Jesus was doing for us in this prayer. He championed us before his Father. Yes, he knew that we as future believers would sin. Yes, he knew that we would not deserve the scholarship of eternal life. Yes, he knew that we would not live up to the name *Christian*. Nonetheless, he interceded on our behalf with his Father—that we would be unified as a body of believers, that we would be with him someday, and that we would love as the Father loved the Son. He knew the church would have significant challenges ahead, even from the time he appointed seventy-two as his advance teams before he visited various towns. Jesus said, "The harvest is plentiful, but the workers are few. Ask the Lord of the harvest, therefore, to send out workers into his harvest field. Go! I am sending you out like lambs among wolves" (Luke 10:2–3). Prayer is critical in ministry, and seeking the Lord of the harvest in prayer for direction, unity, and more is essential for a good harvest for God's kingdom.

The significance of this section of the priestly prayer is that it belongs to two lives and two worlds—the days of Jesus' flesh and the years of his glory. Heaven and earth.[7] The Son in earthly sandals prayed to his "Righteous Father" in heaven. I wonder if Jesus looked into the future and saw me. It makes me wiggle a little to think about his seeing the real me. An angry teenager who ran away from the church when her pastor had an affair with a married woman. A born-again college girl who did not send in her application to the international missions organization because she was afraid of the prospect of raising support. The young mother who didn't follow through with nightly devotions with her children because she was too tired. The prayerwalker who stopped prayerwalking for a long season because of hurt and betrayal. I have failed him so much.

However, Jesus saw all of that junk of mine and more. In that Upper Room as he prayed, he saw your junk, too. Despite our failings, he prayed for us. And despite our hurts and anger and disappointments in others, we can pray for them, too, as our Master Teacher showed us.

PRAYER FOR THE MINISTRY OF THE SAINTS

Father, I pray for unity in my church and its ministries, as well as for the unity of the global Christian church. May we be one as you and your Son are one. Your Spirit dwells inside me, as it dwells inside all who believe. Help us to cancel out the many things that would divide us and instead focus on what we have in common—a love for your Son Jesus Christ and a mission to live our lives in such a way that others are drawn to eternal life through faith in him. Lord, may we someday together see the glory you gave your Son before the creation of the world. There are many specific ways I could pray for my church's ministries, Father, but I simply want to tell you that I will make you known to others by demonstrating your love to other believers and to others who will believe. Be glorified through your church here on earth, Lord, as you were glorified through your Son, Jesus Christ. In his name I pray, amen!

Adapted from John 17:20–26

GROWING IN *Prayer*

1. Why is oneness in the church important?
2. Read John 17:20–21. How does it make you feel when you read that Jesus prayed for all those who would believe in him?

3. While we may all have examples of church-gone-bad moments, what specific examples can you think of that the church has done right?

4. How could we practically live out unity in a church setting? What would that look like in specific ways?

5. What ministries in your church or a parachurch organization demonstrate God's love?

6. How could you pray for a specific church ministry?

7. For what Christian ministry worker(s) could you pray?

Chapter 10

Jesus' Prayer over Critical Decisions

There was one time when I was unable to finish out a teaching year—the literal trial of our lives. In December 2001 my husband, Craig, lost five calves and an old bull after a two-day blizzard. They had bedded down in a dry creek bed, and the snow covered them over. A neighbor, who resented my husband because he would not sell him a strip of his land, saw the dead animals and called not my husband but the local animal control agency. My husband was charged with numerous felony animal-abuse charges—despite the fact that necropsies on two of the animals showed one calf had twenty pounds of feed in its stomach and the other had a high level of colostrum from its mother. It took three and a half years for the case to get to trial—something we thought we'd simply have to live through because the evidence was highly in my husband's favor. However, we did not anticipate that the judge would mock my husband's witnesses in front of the jury, disallow evidence from a cattle auction that showed top dollar for my husband's cattle, and not permit a key witness to testify—a University of California, Davis, veterinary school professor who was considered the beef cattle expert of the West.

Craig was convicted of six felony counts of animal abuse. His two-week-long trial was during the crazy time of my teaching year as the senior class adviser—coaching students through their senior project presentations, planning their senior banquet and scholarship program, and more. I kept teaching during that time, other than one day when I had to testify, trying to keep my composure as the judge continued to interrupt me and mock me: "Who do you think you are, Virginia Woolf, that you go on and on like this?" I was trying to explain how my husband literally brought calves into our home during winter storms when they needed to be warmed up because their moms weren't taking care of them. My kids would say, "Mom, don't go look in the bathroom right now." I knew what would be in the tub—another cute black-and-white calf.

I was also with him when the verdict came back. Guilty. Guilty. Guilty. Guilty. Guilty. Guilty. I watched the back of my husband as he stood there. I saw him flinch with each response as though he'd been shot. I willed myself not to faint, not to retch, not to cry. Other than his attorney, I was the only person in the room who knew he was innocent and that things had gone bizarrely wrong. And I had to drive him home—home until his sentencing two months later.

At home, though, I fell apart. The possibilities were frightening. How would our family function if Craig went to prison for the maximum sentence of three years—or even three months? Who would feed the cattle and take care of the hay farming? Would his cattle be taken away from him? I could not figure out how to put food together for our youngest and us. A friend brought over dinner, but I could not eat. My heart would not stop racing, and I could not imagine going back to work or going into the local grocery or post office. I called in sick to school for the next couple of days and made an appointment with a doctor, who prescribed antidepressants and a leave of absence from teaching through the end of the school year. This was a crisis—and I was not responding well.

Best Human Prayer Is Dichotomous

Jesus, however, did the right thing under crisis. He prayed. After he left the Upper Room, he led the disciples to the garden at Gethsemane, where he prayed, "My Father, if it is possible, may this cup be taken from me. Yet not as I will, but as you will" (Matthew 26:39). A second time he prayed, "My Father, if it is not possible for this cup to be taken away unless I drink it, may your will be done" (Matthew 26:42). Then Scripture tells us he prayed the same thing a third time. The gospel writer Mark recorded a slightly different rendition of Jesus' prayer: "'Abba, Father,' he said, "'everything is possible for you. Take this cup from me. Yet not what I will, but what you will'" (Mark 14:36). Faced with the prospect of dying on a cross, Jesus responded as any human would. However, he also responded with complete trust in his heavenly Father.

This dichotomous prayer is what I call a two-sided-coin prayer.[1] Because we, too, are human, we can know that on the one side, Jesus wanted life. The beatings and crucifixion and pain until death would be excruciating. Even more so Jesus faced the prospect of separation from the Father between the time of death and the time of resurrection. On the other hand, he prayed God's will be done—an honest desire in tandem with the most heavenward prayer. This prayer over all others we will study is the best possible human prayer we can pray. We vulnerably and humbly lay out before God what we would desire at this point in our earthly lives, but give over the right to cancellation of that request if it does not align with God's perfect plan.

Attitude is everything in prayer, as we learn from Jesus' parable of the Pharisee and the tax collector.

"Two men went up to the temple to pray, one a Pharisee and the other a tax collector. The Pharisee stood up and prayed about himself: 'God, I thank you that I am not like other men—robbers, evildoers, adulterers—or even like this tax collector. I fast twice a week and give a tenth of all I get.'

"But the tax collector stood at a distance. He would not even look up to heaven, but beat his breast and said, 'God, have mercy on me, a sinner.'

"I tell you that this man, rather than the other, went home justified before God. For everyone who exalts himself will be humbled, and he who humbles himself will be exalted."

Luke 18:10–14

When we approach God with an I-deserve-this attitude, we are not aligning ourselves with God's perfect plan. Humility puts self last; humility puts God first. And humility understands that God knows best for self.

As the medication began to kick in, that was when I began to surface and pray . . . well, the first half of that prayer, anyway. *Remove this ugly trial from our lives, Lord. Zap it away. I hate this. It hurts, God. Help us. This isn't fair.* But the process continued, and my seniors graduated that year without my being there. As for me, I was still pretty much flattened. I needed help.

Help arrived soon. Dinners were delivered. Friends visited. And the prayer warriors arrived in full force. Even Jesus relied upon those who would join with him in prayer, and taught that prayer partnership was powerful. After he came down off the mountain after the transfiguration and arrived with the disciples back in Galilee, Jesus began a series of teachings. This was one of them:

"I tell you the truth, whatever you bind on earth will be bound in heaven, and whatever you loose on earth will be loosed in heaven.

"Again, I tell you that if two of you on earth agree about anything you ask for, it will be done for you by my Father in heaven. For where two or three come together in my name, there am I with them."

Matthew 18:18–20

Partnership in prayer for life's crises is essential for at least three reasons. First, it provides the opportunity for agreement in prayer. If I am really unable to see God's hand in my life because I'm blocking my own view, my friend who is praying alongside me can provide that perspective. She might be able to point out something I am not seeing so that my *help-me* prayer flips to the other side of the coin, to the *your-will-be-done* side. When we are praying in accord with Jesus' perspective, God's will can be done in our lives.

Another reason for garnering a prayer team around you in crisis times is that we are not meant to bear burdens alone. We draw strength from each other as we pray together. Even Jesus asked the disciples to keep watch in the Gethsemane garden while he prayed, and while they are faulted with falling asleep while Jesus prayed, someone was awake listening to Jesus' prayers, as we have three separate gospel accounts about Jesus pleading with his Father (Matthew, Mark, Luke). While Jesus was accustomed to spending whole evenings on a mountainside or other lonely places praying by himself (Luke 5:16; 6:12), this time Jesus didn't disappear from everyone else—they were nearby, listening or . . . well, some were dozing.

Partnering and Persistence Are Powerful

A third reason for partnering in prayer is that others can step in and persist when we get weary or frustrated in long-term prayer efforts. This was another of Jesus' teachings. Within a string of parables and miracles in the gospel of Luke is the parable of the persistent widow, which Jesus told his disciples "to show them that they should always pray and not give up" (Luke 18:1). In the parable, Jesus said there was a judge who did not fear God and did not care about men (that sounds familiar, reader), to whom a widow kept coming with the plea, "Grant me justice against my adversary" (Luke 18:3). While he did not initially rule in her favor, because she kept persisting with him, he said, "I will see that she gets justice, so that she won't eventually wear me out with her coming!" (Luke 18:5). Jesus provided the application:

> "Listen to what the unjust judge says. And will not God bring about justice for his chosen ones, who cry out to him day and night? Will he keep putting them off? I tell you, he will see that they get justice, and quickly. However, when the Son of Man comes, will he find faith on the earth?"
>
> Luke 18:6–8

Notice here that while our persistence in prayer is rewarded, Jesus is teaching that it is less important that our prayers are answered, and more important that we draw closer to our heavenly Judge as we seek him continually. Prayer is indeed a posture of faith, but our faith should grow commensurately when God answers our prayers.

Persistence in prayer is important. Jesus prayed three times, not just once, for the cup to be taken from him. While a first reading of this passage could imply that we could break God down with our many prayers, a closer reflection teaches that our persistent pursuit breaks us down into a oneness with his will, which has a sovereign design for our lives.

Clearly, the Father does want us to go to him when we are in need. In fact, he teaches this in Matthew 7:

"Ask and it will be given to you; seek and you will find; knock and the door will be opened to you. For everyone who asks receives; he who seeks finds; and to him who knocks, the door will be opened.

"Which of you, if your son asks for bread, will give him a stone? Or if he asks for a fish, will give him a snake? If you, then, though you are evil, know how to give good gifts to your children, how much more will your Father in heaven give good gifts to those who ask him!"

vv. 7–11

Prayer is not a guessing game. Do I have the right words? Do I have the right timing? Do I have the right heart? No worries. We simply go to the Father with the best prayer humanly possible, knowing that he loves us, that he provides for us, and that he has fish for us, not a snake, and bread for us, not a stone. We know how much we love our children and wish the best for them. Similarly, our heavenly Father desires to favor us with his goodness. We simply need to ask, to persist, and to garner a tribe who will pray with us and for us over the long haul.

Such happened with us. People stopped by to pray. People wrote cards. One friend sent me a Scripture promise every single day for the two months between the trial and the sentencing date and beyond. She told me, "You need to know someone is praying for you every day. Post these verses around the house so you know you are not alone. Let them speak truth into you when life is getting dark."

And life was kind of dark during that time, but there was a pinhole of light at the tunnel's end. It took a long time to walk through that tunnel. But I had a hint of how God answers prayer after the sentencing hearing. A whole courtroom of family and friends showed up that day. After getting sick four or five times on the hour-long drive to the courthouse, I found a crowd of smiling faces in the parking lot who walked us in. Six different pastors were among them. The crowd seemed to stun the judge, who had no caustic or sarcastic comments that day. Seemingly, he even stammered, saying he didn't want our son in college to abort his education to take care of the cattle, so he would not give prison time—but *only* four years of probation instead. There was also a huge fine—many times more than what my husband typically earns in a year from his cattle sales.

While my friends were all around me in the courtroom this time, my eyes were completely focused on the back of Craig again. This time he stood up straight and he didn't flinch. I was seeing what the "peace that passeth all understanding" looks like in the flesh, there in my husband's demeanor. So that you understand, my husband is not a smiley guy—he's very shy and usually pretty serious. But that day he was smiling in the courtroom. The power of prayer was not only holding him up; it was giving him joy.

Outside the courthouse the men gathered around my husband, and their wives gathered around me.

"Craig was amazing today," one said.

"What a testimony as a Christian believer," someone else said.

"I so admire him," a third person said.

What? Craig? But when I looked at him, I had to agree. And I fell in love with him all over again . . . the very answer to years of prayer for my attitude about our marriage. *I don't want to be in this marriage, God, but not my will but yours be done.* And right then and there, it was being done, in God's mysterious timing and peculiar circumstances.

I would be remiss if I didn't let you know that we took the case to the California Court of Appeals, handling the appeal ourselves, with detailed evidence from the transcripts about the judge's misdeeds—hundreds of them, documented with references to the transcript. Two years after the trial, the decision was reversed; my husband was a free man, and his records were cleared.

Jesus' prayers in the Gethsemane garden teach us that everything is possible for God. We can ask the Father for anything. We are not limited by our understanding of the laws of nature or the lack of justice on earth or our human thinking. He can do the impossible through and for his finite creation here on earth. Sometimes his answers—even if they're not of our choosing—are better than we could imagine.

It's interesting that the gospel writers chose to relate the fact that the disciples failed to support Jesus prayerfully in the worst crisis moment of his life. He could have chosen to get out of town—to run for his life and hide in the wilderness. He could have torn down columns a la Samson, crushing his religious and secular opponents and making himself king of Israel. After all, that was what the Jews expected—a Messiah who would sit on a literal throne, not one who would die on a cross. He could have done all that . . . except that he also prayed, "Yet not as I will, but as you will" (Matthew 26:39). It's a good thing, too, because what would have happened if the Father had said, "Okay, I'll take that cup away. Just come on home"? What would have been the Salvation Plan B? No, much as Jesus wanted not to face that pain ahead, his greater desire was to fulfill his Father's plan for his life on earth.

When we truly have the desire for God's will in our lives, we can have peace about praying that second half of the perfect prayer. And that can come about more readily with a posse of prayer partners who also have a heart not only for our best but also for God's best for us. If you don't have such a posse, it is time to seek out one or more friends who will persist in prayer with you through the crises of your life. And certainly, those people will need you as well for theirs.

PRAYER OVER CRITICAL DECISIONS

Father, I have a difficult decision to make. I want to do the right thing and need to know the course that you would have me take. Sometimes it is not so clear which way is your way and which way is not. Some might say, "Do whatever seems best to you," but I want to inquire what it is you desire of me. Please give me the right answer, Lord, for on this day I am choosing you as the one I will serve and obey. Your way is the way of truth, and so I will set my heart on your Word and look there for your direction, for your path leads to freedom. Father, I know that you can weigh my heart. You know that I am human and weak and needy. But here I am before you, laying down my human desires for your perfect will in my life, because no matter what my earthly vision is now, I do know that your greater plan in my life will always be better than anything else I could imagine. So this is my prayer: that your love may abound more and more through me and that others may be able to discern Christlikeness through me so that they, too, will know you and that you will be honored and praised. In Jesus' name, amen!

Adapted from Deuteronomy 30:15–16; 1 Samuel 14:36–49;
Joshua 24:15; Psalm 119:30–32; Proverbs 21:2;
Luke 22:42; Philippians 1:9–10

GROWING IN *Prayer*

1. When a crisis hits, how do you typically pray?
2. Read Matthew 26:36–46. What do you think Jesus meant when he asked that the cup be taken from him? What were his choices at that point in his life?

3. How do you view the prayer "Yet not as I will, but as you will"?

4. Read Matthew 7:7–11 and 18:18–20. What do these passages teach about the character of God and how he feels about our prayers and us?

5. What does the parable of the persistent widow (Luke 18:1–8) teach us about persevering in prayer?

6. To what people can you turn when you are in crisis and need prayer support?

7. What is weighing on your heart today? Reach out to a friend who could partner with you in prayer for this need.

Chapter 11

Jesus' Prayer for Forgiveness

Perhaps one of the toughest injustices to get past comes when those you love and have cared for and perhaps have even mentored betray you—a figurative crucifixion, if you will. That happened to me some years ago when a group of students I had coached and encouraged through the college and scholarship application process turned on me, senior class adviser, because they were unhappy about the school's traditional graduation décor. Suddenly I was Public Teacher Enemy Number One and shunned—I, the one who had written countless recommendation letters for them and advocated many times on their behalf with scholarship organizations. Probably the most humiliating teacher moment I experienced over twenty-six years was when I walked down the hall and saw them gathered in T-shirts they had made to mock me. That hurt, and the rest of the year proved emotionally bumpy until I remembered something Jesus prayed on the cross: "Father, forgive them, for they know not what they do" (Luke 23:34 KJV).

If there were only one thematic idea that runs through the New Testament, it would have to be forgiveness. Forgiveness was Jesus' mission, and so it is fitting that the first of his three prayers from the cross focuses on it. By the time Jesus prayed this, Peter—the one who housed him most of the three ministry years—had denied him, and the other disciples seemingly were hiding out. After Jesus was savagely beaten, he was forced to carry his own cross—taken over by Simon from Cyrene—then crucified, "along with the criminals—one on his right, the other on his left" (Luke 23:33). The next verse reads, "Jesus said, 'Father, forgive them, for they do not know what they are doing.' And they divided up his clothes by casting lots" (Luke 23:34).

The most curious word to me in this one-sentence prayer is *them*. To whom was Jesus referring? As an English teacher, I know that a pronoun, such as the word *them* here, should refer back to the last appropriate noun used—its antecedent. If that is true, the word *them* in this context refers back to the two criminals crucified along with him. However, that does not make sense, as the criminals were not doing anything wrong at that point—their deeds had already been done, and Jesus could have prayed, "Father, forgive them, for they *did* not know what they *were* doing." The logical assumption is that Jesus was praying for the Romans who right then were hammering the nails into his wrists and feet. Certainly, they were just doing their job— executing orders handed down from Roman governor Pontius Pilate. However, there could be a broader *they*: those who had crucified him, those who had forced him to carry his own cross, those who had beaten him, those who had cried "Crucify him! Crucify him!" as well as those who tried him and arrested him and perhaps even betrayed him, or denied him or hid in the shadows instead of standing by him. Many of those might have fully understood what they were doing, but out of cowardice or jealousy they simply did not intervene for him. So in the *least*, Jesus was praying for the soldiers carrying out orders.

Even with that settled we still are left with what may be the most curious of Jesus' prayers: "Father, forgive them, for they do not know what they are doing." This is the Son asking the Father to carry out what he was sent to do—save the world from its sinful separation from God. Jesus' prayer is intercessory on behalf of those who needed mercy—forgiveness even though the soldiers continued their hammering. Jesus prayed, "Give them slack, Father. They don't get it." Certainly if gospel writer Luke heard Jesus' prayer, the hammering soldiers did. You would think his words pierced their hearts, except that in the next beat we learn that they divided up Jesus' clothes by casting lots.

Power Pray

There is tremendous power in forgiveness. I always looked for a teaching moment on that subject when I was in the classroom—either in front of the class or personally with an individual student. I'd say, "So, if you're angry at your friend because of something he has done, who has the power in that situation?" Students always answered quickly, "I do." And I'd respond, "Are you sure? Then why do you say, '*That person* makes me mad'? Do you have control if the other person is still triggering anger in you?" I would allow a pregnant pause to occur—always a great teaching strategy to make others think. Slowly, the light would begin to filter onto their faces, but before a hand would go up, I'd add, "How about if you decide to forgive that person? Who has the power then?" When we forgive, we not only have control or power over the situation and relationship but also have gifted ourselves with freedom from the burden of anger, hatred, and bitterness—all of which can destroy people emotionally and damage the witness of Christ in our lives.

This is not a random teaching on forgiveness in regard to prayer. It was also a key element in the Lord's Prayer: "Forgive us our debts, as we also have forgiven our debtors" (Matthew 6:12). Following that model prayer Jesus added the explanation, "For if you forgive men when they sin against you, your heavenly Father will also forgive you. But if you do not forgive men their sins, your Father will not forgive your sins" (Matthew 6:14–15). Forgiveness is reciprocal: If we expect to get it, we should give it. While Jesus did not need forgiveness for himself, he would not deny it for others. It was why he was lying there on that cross with his hands and feet being hammered with iron stakes.

Forgiveness prayer is not just a once-in-a-lifetime prayer; it's something we should do daily—certainly praying that God would forgive us, and giving our forgiveness to others—but there's another element: praying for God's forgiveness of the person who has wronged us. This kind of prayer, effectively, is for that person's salvation—a Jesus kind of prayer. You can certainly ask forgiveness for yourself from God, but when you want eternity changed, you pray, "Father, forgive them, for they know not what they do." Those who-do-not-know-what-they-do need the most prayer, after all.

The power in forgiveness makes a kingdom of difference. Jesus makes this point while teaching about faith.

"Have faith in God," Jesus answered. "I tell you the truth, if anyone says to this mountain, 'Go, throw yourself into the sea,' and does not doubt in his heart but believes that what he says will happen, it will be done for him. Therefore I tell you, whatever you ask for in prayer, believe that you have received it, and it will be yours. And when you stand praying, if you hold anything against anyone, forgive him, so that your Father in heaven may forgive you your sins."

Mark 11:22–26

As we pray, God will nudge us about not only sins we have committed but also resentments we hold against others. Our forgiveness of others, Jesus teaches here, is tied to his forgiveness of us—but also could lead to others being led to faith as they see our humble faith posture.

No other faith teaches people to pray for their enemies. That makes Christianity—and God—look good, and that's our job, to show off God. I mean, who wouldn't want debt cancelled, just like that? Such a deal! God can forgive even the greatest of sinners, as we learn when Jesus tells the criminal who expresses belief in him, "Today you will be with me in paradise" (Luke 23:43). After the resurrection when Jesus was proving who he was to the disbelieving disciples, he continued to teach them about forgiveness: "If you forgive anyone his sins, they are forgiven; if you do not forgive them, they are not forgiven" (John 20:23). That's the power of forgiveness—someone's life-despite-death experience. Our praying for our enemies' forgiveness could be key in their journey toward faith. When Christian men and women forgive those who do not deserve forgiveness, such a merciful gift could help them understand the forgiveness our Father God offers. While we are not in the business of salvation (the Lord is), if our actions point others heavenward, well, how lovely to have played a small part here on earth!

Among Jesus' teachings in the Sermon on the Mount—where we find the Lord's Prayer—he elaborates on the idea of praying for one's enemies:

> "But I tell you who hear me: Love your enemies, do good to those who hate you, bless those who curse you, pray for those who mistreat you. If someone strikes you on one cheek, turn to him the other also. If someone takes your cloak, do not stop him from taking your tunic. Give to everyone who asks you, and if anyone takes what belongs to you, do not demand it back. Do to others as you would have them do to you.

"If you love those who love you, what credit is that to you? Even 'sinners' love those who love them. And if you do good to those who are good to you, what credit is that to you? Even 'sinners' do that. And if you lend to those from whom you expect repayment, what credit is that to you? Even 'sinners' lend to 'sinners,' expecting to be repaid in full. But love your enemies, do good to them, and lend to them without expecting to get anything back. Then your reward will be great, and you will be sons of the Most High, because he is kind to the ungrateful and wicked. Be merciful, just as your Father is merciful."

Luke 6:27–36

Jesus flipped the eye-for-an-eye rule. We aren't allowed the margin to pray for some and not for others. Our love for God should drive us to love—and thus forgive—others, not hold on to grudges that destroy relationships and impede our witness. Jesus had compassion on his crucifiers. The Father is an equal opportunity employer for heaven's kingdom: Both good people and evil people can receive forgiveness. There's no room for payback. Each of us makes a faith choice, which has a heaven-or-hell kind of consequence.

Bridging the Divide

There are several ways we can seek forgiveness, all of which can relate to prayer. First, when we've done something wrong that affects no one else (which usually is doubtful), we simply ask God to forgive us. If we are believers, essentially we are forgiven eternally, but it's important to own up to our disobedience and debts with God. *Father, I knew I should not have overeaten. I feel sick, literally, but I also know that I have disappointed you and that when I choose to indulge myself, I am not honoring you. Thank you for forgiving me.*

Another type of forgiveness prayer is when our sin affects both God and someone else. When we hurt someone, we ask God to forgive us, but we also have to make it right with the other person. Jesus addresses this in Matthew 5:23–24:

> "Therefore, if you are offering your gift at the altar and there remember that your brother has something against you, leave your gift in front of the altar. First go and be reconciled to your brother; then come and offer your gift."

So we pray for God's forgiveness, but we also seek out that person or persons to say something like this: "I was wrong when I made that unkind remark to you the other day. Will you forgive me?" Admitting responsibility is humbling and is more restorative for the relationship, so just saying "Sorry" is not enough. I believe God must smile when his people humble themselves. That is a moment when God is glorified and when others can see that our faith works in such a way to transform our lives and bring peace to the world.

A final kind of forgiveness prayer occurs when we have been offended: "Father, forgive them, for they know not what they do." The Jesus-on-the-cross prayer—the first thing he took care of prayer-wise from that horrible position of humility. From the lowliest posture, this prayer brings honor and glory to God. While others might curse in anger, the Jesus student follows the lead of his Master Teacher, forgives that person, and asks his heavenly Father to forgive him as well. It's a two-pronged prayer: *Father, I forgive this person for trying to destroy my reputation, and I ask you to forgive him as well.*

A curse is broken when the Christian prays for forgiveness. Sin can divide people when they react with anger instead of a turn of the cheek. The enemy has a foothold at this point, creating a greater divide as the parties rant to anyone who will listen, who then allow the parties to justify what they've said or done. A river of bitterness turns the narrow canyon into a widened gorge, separating the people even farther from each other . . . and from God. Words get thrown around more—and families and communities and even churches experience division that seems irreparable. But when that cross of forgiveness is extended from one side of the chasm to the other, there is then a bridge that breaks the curse of separation.

It is extremely hard to take the high road when others have hurt us. In my situation at school with the senior students, I so wanted to go to my administrator and whine about how mean they were being to me. But I'm the adult, and I know that is how students typically react—hallway drama, they call it. So instead I blinked back tears, smiled, held my head up, and treated them no differently than I had in the past. *Father, forgive them, for they know not how bad I feel.* I figured that someday they might look back on that incident and regret it—but perhaps not. In any case, we finished out the year with a fabulous community service project of planting thirty-three large trees in the city park, an all-day job of which we were all proud as we dug holes, put in soil amendments, and planted each tree, packing it soundly and watering it. Well, I just supervised, I must admit, but I didn't even have to nudge them. They worked really hard, and I was super proud of each one. Together we accomplished a lot that year, and they stepped up to the many challenges in an adult fashion.

Forgiveness is Christian faith in action. This is what draws people in. We all make mistakes. We all say dumb things. Hurting people hurt people. However, Jesus-followers own up to their failures and pray for and seek forgiveness, which is the chief distinction between the faith we profess and the other religions of the world. Christianity is all about relationship—the eternal, personal relationship with the God of the universe. We are forgiven because of Christ. So we pray forgiveness as our Prayer Mentor has taught us, so that others will come into relationship with him as well.

PRAYER FOR FORGIVENESS

Lord, I have been greatly offended and hurt by someone. I no longer want this conflict to come between us and between you and me. Forgive me, Lord, for the anger and bitterness I have allowed to creep into my soul. With your strength and guidance I forgive this person and commit to making every attempt to be reconciled. Your Word says that if I do not forgive others, I should not expect to receive your forgiveness. Thank you for your graceful, even merciful, forgiveness, Lord. Even if this person hurts me again, I will continue to forgive, because your Son said that we should forgive seventy times seven, and that our forgiveness should not just be in words but from our hearts. Thank you for your teaching that we should not only forgive but also offer comfort, so that the other person is not overwhelmed by excessive sorrow. Offenses can create division of the Christian body, Lord, so I will do what I can to restore this relationship and model unity for your sake and for the sake of your kingdom. In Jesus' name, amen!

Adapted from Matthew 5:23–24; 6:12–15;
18:21–35; 2 Corinthians 2:5–11

GROWING IN *Prayer*

1. Why do people so easily expect to be forgiven, yet find it so hard to seek that forgiveness from others for things they do wrong?

2. Read Luke 23:26–34. What would be going through your mind if you were in Jesus' position?

3. How is forgiveness kingdom work?

4. Have you ever prayed for an enemy? Did your prayers effect a change in your relationship? Did they change you?

5. Should we pray for those who hurt us, even if they are aware of the hurt they are causing? How would you feel about that?

6. How does Luke 6:31 relate to prayer?

7. Think of someone who needs your or God's forgiveness and pray for that person now.

Chapter 12

Jesus' Prayer in Abandonment

Many times I saw hopelessness in the faces of my students, and many times those students were victims of abuse. One girl had coat-hanger scratches all over. Another girl was sleeping on a friend's couch because her mom's boyfriend was hitting her. There were many sad stories, all of which I referred to child protective services. The worst was a girl who went missing for more than a day, then finally came to school and confided in me.

"Don't tell my parents, please," she said. "My dad will have a fit."

She explained that she had gotten a ride to visit a friend, who had been hospitalized in Reno, about an hour from our town. The young man's father and brother volunteered to drive her home but instead took her to their home, where they assaulted her. Once I knew that, I had to report the case, which brought her parents into the picture. The hardest part for me, however, was hearing her father tell her that he wanted to leave her to fend for herself. Instead of rescuing her, he wanted to abandon her.

Jesus was abandoned, too, and perhaps his most painful prayer is his second one from the cross:[1]

> From the sixth hour until the ninth hour darkness came over all the land. About the ninth hour Jesus cried out in a loud voice, "*Eloi, Eloi, lama sabachthani?*"—which means, "My God, my God, why have you forsaken me?"
>
> Matthew 27:45–46

The agonizing poignancies strike us. The common address of "Father" is not found here, but instead there is a personalized "My God, my God"—not an impersonal address but a hurting-heart one. While Jesus often used the word *why* in his instruction of his disciples, now the question is addressed to his Father. And the word *forsaken* takes on such a note of finality for the hearers—not only for Jesus' time on earth, but also for his relationship with his Father.

This prayer above all others may be Jesus' most agonizing, because it addresses the biggest, most often asked question mankind has about God. *Why.* Why does God allow suffering? Why must we fall into the hellholes of life? If God loves us so much, wouldn't such a loving Father steer us around the intersections of pain? Wouldn't there be a better way? Like me, you might wonder what Jesus was thinking as he was facing death. Was he afraid? Would he be completely separated from his Father in his death experience? Was he already sensing that as he hung on the cross?

Jesus was actually reciting a verse from Psalm 22. It is possible that Jesus may have recited the whole psalm and that only the one verse was recorded by the gospel writer. David penned that psalm after experiencing cruel and seemingly unending attacks by enemies he had not provoked and from whom the Lord had not yet delivered him.[2] No other psalm, perhaps, fit Jesus' crucifixion circumstances so exactly, with the psalm continuing like this:

> Why are you so far from saving me,
>   so far from the words of my groaning?
> O my God, I cry out by day, but you do not answer,
>   by night, and am not silent.
>
> Psalm 22:1–2

Clearly, Jesus felt his Father had abandoned him as he bore the sins of mankind as a final sacrifice.

This psalm was the one most frequently quoted by New Testament writers, a lament that seemingly crept into conversation much in the same way we quote Psalm 23 today: "The Lord is my shepherd, I shall not be in want. . . ."[3] How better to face fear than to quote Scripture? I have had several MRI procedures over the years. Each time as I slid into the claustrophobia-inducing tube, I closed my eyes and silently repeated Psalm 23 over and over again. Jesus shows us here that we do not have to come up with the words when the earth is crashing down on us. We can pray using Scripture—such as the laments of the psalms.

When my husband and I were awaiting his sentencing years ago, however, I could not even read the Bible. The words seemed to melt into gray matter on the page. I did find great comfort, though, in the profound devotional book *Streams in the Desert* by L. B. Cowman. During the two months between the end of the trial and the sentencing, I read the entire yearlong book of daily devotions, underlining sentences that spoke life to me as the writer reflected on verses from Scripture. On the hour-long drive from our home to the courthouse, I read aloud those passages as though they were our own prayer promises, such as the following:

> Yet the land we are to possess is a land of valleys and hills. It is not all flat or downhill. . . . We need the valleys *and* the hills. The hills collect the rain for hundreds of fruitful valleys. And so it is with us! It is the difficulty encountered on the hills that drives us to the throne of grace and brings the showers of blessing.

Yes, it is the hills, the cold and seemingly barren hills of life that we question and complain about, that bring down the showers. How many people have perished in the wilderness valley, buried under its golden sand, who would have thrived in the hills? And how many would have been killed by the cold, destroyed or swept desolate of their fruitfulness by the wind, if not for the hills—stern, hard, rugged, and so steep to climb? God's hills are a gracious protection for His people against their foes![4]

But before that day of sentencing we had a lot of *whys*. We, too, felt forsaken.

A Greater Plan

We don't use the word *forsaken* much in our conversational language. We say "abandoned" or "deserted" or the colloquial "dumped." We can thank Matthew and Mark for translating from an Aramaic dialect to the Greek word *enkataleipō*, which means "to abandon, leave in straits"—with an implied sense of helplessness.[5] Jesus was not a liar or an actor playing a part, and so when he prayed his "why," he certainly was alone on that cross—not just experiencing a feeling of abandonment.

He was appealing to God as the final King of the eternal court of justice. Just as Craig and I took our case eventually to an appellate court, so did Jesus. He appealed to the Judge on High. Was it fair that Jesus would have to suffer? No, he did no wrong. Were the charges against him correct? No, he truly was the Messiah, the Son of the living God—not simply claiming to be the Christ. Should he have been there? No, those who had followed him and were healed by him should have testified in his behalf. So Jesus was experiencing—in the extreme—the anguish every human has experienced, the life-is-not-fair moment. And he appealed to his Father's court on high—the God of the Old Testament who righted wrongs, who defended Israel, and who protected those who followed him. The "My God" Father would know that the testimony was false, and he could make the wrong right again. He would hear the "whys" of Jesus' cries and deliver him.

But he did not. Life was not fair for Jesus. Even though he was popular with the people, sought after by thousands, and even praised as a king just one day before his crucifixion, there was no last-minute reprieve. There was no stay of execution. There was no *deus ex machina*. (In literature, when characters are seemingly helpless and in a horrible climactic disaster but all of a sudden are saved through an unexpected plot device, that is called *deus ex machina*, or "god of the machine.") A classic example of *deus ex machina* is seen at the end of the novel *Lord of the Flies* by William Golding, when a naval officer suddenly appears on the deserted island and saves the British schoolboys from certain self-destruction. In the movie theater we might clap and cheer because the officer saved the day.

That's what we would expect the save-the-day God of the Old Testament to do: rescue Jesus and show everyone that miracles happen big-time when God is involved. But there was no parting of the Red Sea. There was no rainstorm to end the drought. There was no fast food miracle to feed five thousand people with a couple of fish and a few loaves of bread. Jesus was forsaken by the Father. Jesus would continue to hang on the cross and die there. And the Judge remained silent through it all. Jesus was abandoned.

Every once in a while a story hits the news about a baby being abandoned on church steps or some other public place. Our hearts ache for such a helpless little boy or girl. We wonder why parents would go to such extreme measures. What life circumstances were they going through? Were they unwed? Were they poor? Were they drug addicted? Were they uneducated about the legal system and adoption process? Were they overwhelmed by pressures of life? Or were they simply embarrassed or even

143

irresponsible? The ultimate in helplessness is seen in the abandonment of a newborn child.

We wait anxiously for the happily-ever-after story. Would the firefighter or the preacher swoop up that baby and claim it? Even better, perhaps a couple who had waited through years of infertility would be in the right spot in the adoption process to take the child home. Their prayers would be answered when a panicked, ill-equipped single mother abandoned her child. The new parents would choose the forsaken one, and a seemingly hopeless situation would turn into one that would bring great joy and purpose.

Such was the case with Jesus. He had to experience his Father's abandonment of him so that others would find him and claim him as their own. That was the greater plan. The seemingly hopeless situation of the Cross, wherein the Father let go his grip of the Son's hand, has since then led to the adoption of untold-on-earth numbers of those who would believe Jesus Christ was truly the Son of God, incarnate of the Father, as the Savior of the world. Christ's cries were heard by the just Judge, but he would not intervene in the sovereign plan to save his Son, because instead he would provide a means of salvation for each of his beloved—each one of us. As a parent I cannot imagine how the Father handled watching his suffering Son. I was one of those helicopter parents who swooped in to save my kids the slightest heartache, even though those heartaches could have led to a greater lesson. But the Father knew better. His forsaken Son brought about the adoption of you. His abandonment led to your acceptance into the loving embrace of the Father. Abandonment led to your adoption.

Praying through Our "Why"

Our "why" prayers are not insignificant. They breathe out humanity in the Father's direction. They are not a lack of faith;

they are simply a lack of information. We do not yet know God's purpose in our suffering. It simply is, and that's all we can see for the moment. We are a feeling people. We feel alone. We feel uncared for. We feel rejected. However, God—even in his silence to our "whys"—is still at work. He is about to do something greater than save us from our trial. He is working out a greater good.

My student who was sexually assaulted did find her happily-ever-after. Her parents eventually rallied around her. Her father rededicated his life to Christ and went on to study at a Bible school to become a pastor. She herself married and has several children. The pain of her past was redeemed in new life. Such could be true of us, too, when we cry, "My God, my God, why have you forsaken me?"

My students from years ago dearly loved a woman from my town who owned a local video store that also sold paraphernalia for skateboarders. You know, things like "SKATEBOARDING IS NOT A CRIME" bumper stickers. I prayed for her as I prayerwalked past her little store. I should not have been surprised when she showed up at church one Sunday morning and made a profession of faith shortly afterward. As it turns out, though, as one of the chief proponents of a skate park in our town, she was not skating through life herself: She was suffering from Stage 4 cancer and did not live very long after that. It did not seem fair to my students or me. However, her death actually caused many to rally together to raise funds in her honor. We now have a skate park in our city park—a facility that my former-city-councilman husband says is still the most-used feature of that park. Diane's dark night of the soul turned into a bright spot faith-wise not only for her but also for the young people in my community.[6]

Because Jesus prayed this seemingly dark "why" prayer, we can, too. We are allowed to struggle in prayer. We are permitted to cry and complain. We may question our Father. We may lament the what-is and wish for a should-be. Our going to the

Father in such a time indicates our faith—that he is the source of our faith and that he is the almighty One who can handle not only the seemingly impossible but also our struggles with it. All of that will lead to light. Jesus knew his purpose. He knew his abandonment would lead to our adoption. The mystic Saint John of the Cross wrote about relationship between the dark and the light in his work *Dark Night of the Soul*:

> It now remains to be said that, although this happy night brings darkness to the spirit, it does so only to give it light in everything; and that, although it humbles it and makes it miserable, it does so only to exalt it and to raise it up; and, although it impoverishes it and empties it of all natural affection and attachment, it does so only that it may enable it to stretch forward, divinely, and thus to have fruition. . . .[7]

Our dark and miserable state may be an important element in a greater work of light and fruition that God has ordained because of our faith and obedience.

We may have those dark nights of the soul when we feel there is no better solution than to pray, *Save me now, Lord!* Our suffering is being viewed from a raised platform. Others are watching to see how Christians suffer. Yes, we pray, *My God, my God, why have you forsaken me?* And that's all right, because it helps others see our humanity—so they can identify with us. We need not be a superhero, unfazed by pain and suffering. Jesus' "why" prayer gives us permission to pray, *Why?* Such a prayer does not indicate our lack of faith; it merely indicates our humanity. The important thing is that we pray—that we turn to God in the dark times. The immediate answer may not always be pretty, but we can trust in the final words that the resurrected Jesus spoke to his disciples before joining his Father in heaven: "And surely I am with you always, to the very end of the age." In other words, Jesus will not forsake you.

PRAYER FOR MOMENTS OF DESPAIR

Lord, I am going through some really hard times right now. I pray that I remain faithful to you throughout the days ahead, so that my witness brings glory to you. You know what lies before me and are in charge of the whole world, so I trust you for my future. Your eyes are on me—as are others, I am sure—so guide my walk when I falter, Lord. You are not an absent Creator—you show up and coach us through our suffering. When I cannot sleep, I will seek out your songs in the night to remind me that you have equipped me for this very time. Remind me of your commands and teachings written on the tablet of my heart so that I do not fall away and allow doubt and despair to run my life. May I come out of this time of testing a refined believer, so that others see that faith works in the furnace of life . . . and that you lead us out of despair to springs of water that refresh us. In the meantime, help me bear my sorrows and heal my brokenness, so that I can confidently proclaim that you are by my side. Help me not to question the "whys," because I know that my thoughts are not your thoughts, my ways are not your ways, and your eternal purpose behind these struggles is beyond what I can guess. I will consider it all joy to walk through these days ahead, knowing that the testing of my faith will bring about spiritual fruit in my life. Therefore, I pray, Not my will, but yours, Father. In Jesus' name, amen.

Adapted from John 11:4; Psalm 23:3; 34:13–21;
35:10–11; Proverbs 3:3; Isaiah 49:10; 55:8;
James 1:2–5; Matthew 26:39

GROWING IN *Prayer*

1. Describe a time when you felt forsaken or abandoned.

2. Read Matthew 27:45–46. How do you react to this?

3. What kinds of thoughts do people have when they are at a point of despair?

4. Why do we have "why" questions? If we knew the answers to the "whys" of life, do you think that would help us while we are going through a time of suffering? Explain your answer.

5. Read Psalm 22. What verses do you think would have resonated with Jesus in his suffering? To which do you relate?

6. As presented in this chapter, what is the relationship between the abandonment of Christ by the Father and his adoption of new believers?

7. How could you pray now for yourself or others who may feel abandoned in their suffering?

Chapter 13

Jesus' Prayer of Submission

When parents hand over their precious five-year-olds to their kindergarten teachers, it is an emotional experience. The child is excited about wearing new school clothes and carrying his or her very own superhero or princess lunch box, and Mom takes photos on the front porch. But eventually the child may shed some tears at the classroom, and Mom and Dad may shed some back at the car. It's understandable. They are putting their child's life into the hands of an educator, entrusting that teacher with the child's safety and well-being, as well as his or her education. Entrusting someone else with your life is a tenuous proposition . . . unless you have complete faith in that person as someone who has your best interests in mind.

Through prayer, Jesus showed us how to entrust the Father with our very lives.

It was now about the sixth hour, and darkness came over the whole land until the ninth hour, for the sun stopped shining.

And the curtain of the temple was torn in two. Jesus called out with a loud voice, "Father, into your hands I commit my spirit." When he had said this, he breathed his last.

Luke 23:44–46

Only Luke recorded the actual prayer. Two other gospel writers, Matthew and Mark, wrote that Jesus cried out in a loud voice and either "gave up his spirit" (Matthew 27:50) or "breathed his last" (Mark 15:37). John wrote that Jesus' final words were "It is finished" (John 19:30). Indeed, Jesus' life on earth was finished with his final redemptive act that would lead others to eternity. Two days later with his resurrection, the world would be changed forever, with a new understanding that it is possible to have a personal relationship with the living God—not just in heaven but also on earth.

Jesus again addressed the Father tenderly with the use of "Father," the One he had been with since before creation, the One who had sent him, whose hands he trusted and into whose hands he would commit his earthly life. And the Father's hands are worthy of our trust. If we were to repeat Jesus' prayer for ourselves, the Father's hands would be a safe place. God covered Moses with his hand when his glory passed by him—otherwise Moses would have been destroyed by such a display (Exodus 33:22). Everything we have comes from his hand (1 Chronicles 29:14), and anything we have achieved has been accomplished through God's hands (Psalm 44:3). Through his hand, God fulfills all his promises (2 Chronicles 6:15). If those who follow him begin to stumble, he steadies us with his hand (Psalm 37:24). And God's hands are powerful and majestic, able to work miracles for us as he did in bringing the Hebrews out of slavery in Egypt (Exodus 13:3). In fact, we are engraved on the palms of God's hands (Isaiah 49:16). If we pray "Father, into your hands," that will always be a good, good prayer, because we have a good, good Father.

Strength through Release

With this prayer Jesus was once more quoting Scripture, Psalm 31:5, which reads, "Into your hands I commit my spirit; redeem me, O Lord, the God of truth." The Hebrew word for *commit* here means "to deposit," such as you deposit money into your account at your bank, or you deposit your children at the school's front doors.[1] David, the psalm pray-er, entrusted his Father and deposited his very life to God's care, as did Jesus on the cross. This prayer cannot be uttered, though, unless we are fully committed to Christ.

Jesus prayed, "I commit my spirit." The Greek word for *commit* is *paradidōmi*, which is also translated in other versions of the Bible (King James Version and American Standard Version) as *commend* or "to give or deliver over" something.[2] When I write a letter of recommendation for a student, I start by saying, "I *commend* to you Sally Jones, who is a hardworking student with the following positive characteristics. . . ." We commit to a responsibility or commend our children to the Lord when we dedicate them in church. Other translations use the word *entrust* (New Living Translation and Holman) or "to give trust." *I trust you with this.*

I remember when I was given a teaching contract with this assignment: English 8, California History, U.S. History, Life Science 8 (really?), Gifted and Talented. I was stunned that more than one person believed I could do all that. The first day, one science student, who must have known I was an English teacher in disguise, said, "Mrs. McHenry, can you tell me what DNA stands for?"

Without missing a beat I said, "Deoxyribonucleic acid. Now let's figure out what that has to do with us." Then I breathed a sigh of relief, as that was about the only thing I remembered from my single college science course.

Later that week another boy handed me a pillowcase. "What's this?" I said, holding it as far away as possible. I had suspicions. "A snake," he said. "The other science teacher gave us extra credit if we brought in dead animals."

Relieved to hear it was dead, I said, "Well, just put him in the freezer then. And you get extra credit."

A month later a real science teacher was hired, but the whole time I was teaching it, I marveled that people had believed a journalism major could not only teach English but also history courses and life science, for goodness' sake. But I worked hard to prove I was worthy of that trust.

The thing with praying "Into your hands I commit myself" is that this is not a scary prayer. While I may have been masquerading as a science or even history teacher, the God receiving our prayer is no fraud. He created you. He knows everything about you. He knows your situation and your feelings and your struggles. He also knows your future and how your very situation right now—as hard as it might be—is within his sovereign plan for your life. And our Master Teacher and that plan are trustworthy.

Do you love word pictures? *The Aramaic Bible in Plain English* has what I think is a more visual translation of Luke 23:46: "And Yeshua called out in a loud voice and he said, 'My Father, into your hands I lay down my spirit.' He said this and he expired." This helped me visualize Jesus handing himself over into the Father's hands, like that mother relinquishing her child on the first day of kindergarten into the figurative hands of the teacher.

Richard Foster writes of the prayer of relinquishment:

As we are learning to pray we discover an interesting progression. In the beginning our will is in struggle with God's will. We beg. We pout. We demand. We expect God to perform like a magician or shower us with blessings like Father Christmas. We major in instant solutions and manipulative prayers. . . .

In time, however, we begin to enter into a grace-filled releasing of our will and a flowing into the will of the Father. It is the Prayer of Relinquishment that moves us from the struggling to the releasing.[3]

The struggle is real. We have been raised to be strong, independent, Go-West-Young-Man pioneers. From the time we were kindergarteners, others have asked us, "What do you want to be when you grow up?" and we were expected to have answers and a path all lined up directly toward that life goal. It takes time for us to learn that we might not have understood what is best for our lives. We messed up. We hurt people. We made wrong choices with tough consequences.

But as we grow in the faith, we learn that releasing is not a bad thing. There is less anxiety. There are fewer tummy pains and headaches. There is less dependency on substances or a litany of adrenaline experiences to fulfill us and give our lives meaning. Releasing oneself into the Father's hands is not meant only for times of crucifixion; it is a prayer meant for our everyday walk. A prayer of submission actually is an act of strength.

Submission is stronger than resignation. It means more than "I give up, Lord"; it says, "Because I trust you with everything, I commit my life to you." It prays like this: *I give myself over to you because you know what is best for me. I can do nothing more. I need do nothing more. However, I know you ARE the more. My will is simply to give you my life and have you work through me in such a way that you are honored and glorified.*

Jesus had choices. He could have saved himself. He had raised three people from the dead—Lazarus, the daughter of Jairus, and the widow's son at Nain—but he chose himself to be the Suffering Servant. The death accounts of Luke, Matthew, and Mark all record that Jesus cried out loudly just before his death. Luke wrote that he "called out with a loud voice" (Luke 23:46). Jesus died sooner than others did who were crucified, but he had been savagely beaten first. His prayer of relinquishment at the ninth hour before Passover was in sync with the usual hour for prayer as well as the usual time to slay the Passover sacrifice. He submitted himself to be the final Passover lamb. The strength of his cry was a herald that the prophecies had been fulfilled, that the Messiah had come, and that the final sacrifice had been offered up. No more lambs needed to be slain for the sins of mankind. His body and his blood were the final offering.

Only John recorded Jesus' final words: "It is finished" (John 19:30). And those final words shook the world, as well they should have. After all, darkness fell over the land from noon until three o'clock (Luke 23:44–45). The curtain of the temple was torn in two (Luke 23:45; Mark 15:38). And the centurion took note. He was the Roman official, a commander of one hundred men, who was in charge of the crucifixion. His observations and testimonies, then, would have been important, and Luke wrote, "The centurion, seeing what had happened, praised God and said, 'Surely this was a righteous man'" (Luke 23:47). Jesus' prayers on the cross and final words impacted others as well:

> When all the people who had gathered to witness this sight saw what took place, they beat their breasts and went away. But all those who knew him, including the women who had followed him from Galilee, stood at a distance, watching these things.
>
> Luke 23:48–49

Our words matter. Our heartfelt prayers matter. The Father in heaven hears them, and they can affect others on earth. While Jesus said, "It is finished," which could also be viewed as a prayer, he died as a victor. He didn't scream hateful epithets. He didn't curse the soldiers who had nailed him to the tree. He also didn't pray, "Bless me. Favor me. Save me!" No, he had completed what he had come to earth to do, and while he certainly was the final Paschal Lamb, his last prayerful words demonstrate how to give up ourselves to kingdom work. You see, submission occurs through prayer, but obedience must work in tandem. Obedience is the great follow-up act. Christ modeled how prayer can allow the Father to do his greatest resurrection work in our own lives.

Living Out Submission

Jesus offered himself, but we can, too. *Here I am, Lord. Use me.* Our lives can be a prayerful vehicle for God's work on earth. *Into your hands I commend my whole self—my body, my heart, my mind, my spirit.* Jesus' three-year walk toward the cross still shows us how to commit ourselves wholly to God for his continued redemptive plan. Others today could still say of us, "Surely she is a Christ follower," and then ask how one also enters into a relationship with God. I think those conversations can come as a result of a sincere prayer of submission.

As an English teacher, I found that classroom conversations often circled around to faith topics. After all, my juniors studied the works of many Christian writers such as colonial poet Anne Bradstreet and the fiery preacher Jonathan Edwards, and my seniors read works by English poet Christina Rossetti and *A Christmas Carol*, the novella by Charles Dickens, which as we know ends with the words, "God bless Us, Every One!" I never started faith discussions—they happened as a result of the literature approved by the California Department of Education.

I never initiated personal conversations about spiritual topics, either, but students often did with me, one-on-one. Many of those occurred after the horrible events of 9/11. I will never forget one boy asking me, "Mrs. McHenry, do you think this is the end of the world? Is this the beginning of Armageddon?"

I took a deep breath and said, "I do not know. However, I do know that I am ready."

He looked at me for several long moments. "Is that because of your faith, Mrs. McHenry?"

"Yes, Ted, it is."

We had local pastors available in our school at that time to talk with students about the images they had seen on television and the fears that were overwhelming them. So "Ted" went to the library and had a life-changing conversation that day.

While our prayers should be private, our faith should be worn publicly. We need not neon-sign our beliefs to the world if we have submitted our lives to Jesus Christ. The things we say and do make it clear to others that we are Christ followers.

Jesus' final prayer on the cross is reminiscent of the first recorded words of the Savior—those from his childhood, exactly twenty-one years earlier at the time of the Passover (see Luke 2:41–52). As was the custom, his parents, Joseph and Mary, took the family (Jesus and the later-born siblings) to Jerusalem for the celebration of the feast. A day after leaving Jerusalem for home, they realized that the twelve-year-old boy was not among the friends and relatives traveling with them. After they got back to Jerusalem, they found him in the temple courts, "sitting among the teachers, listening to them and asking them questions" (Luke 2:46). When his parents saw that others were impressed by his understanding and answers, they, too, were astonished.

His mother said, "Son, why have you treated us like this? Your father and I have been anxiously searching for you."

His answer foreshadowed what would come: "Why were you searching for me? Didn't you know I had to be in my Father's house?"

That was the thing: Jesus had to be in his Father's house. He was in his Father's house as a twelve-year-old boy, learning the Scriptures. He was in his Father's house healing the sick and resurrecting the dead. He was in his Father's house teaching on the hillsides of Galilee. And he was in his Father's house right there on the cross . . . as he is now resurrected in heaven. We, too, have a choice to be in our Father's house. That comes through a prayer of submission and then the follow-up, prayerful acts of obedience.

PRAYER FOR SUBMISSION

Father, into your hands I commit my life—my heart, my mind, my physical body, and my spirit. I recognize that your sovereign way for my life is better than any design I could imagine, and so I submit myself to the path you have set before me, even if that means there are rocks and valleys and twists along the way. Your lordship in my life is more desirable than success or fame or fortune. I also commit myself to the study of your Word, so that I can better understand what is right and true and what is not. My heart is fully committed to you and your will for the days and years ahead. That includes my family and my interactions with them, my daily work, my finances and money-related decisions, my home and the things I own, my time and time-related decisions, my fellowship with other believers, and my leisure activities. I give myself as a servant through ministry in my church and any other Christian organizations to which you would lead me, as I am committed to living out my life in such a way that others would see you in me. Additionally, it is my desire to submit to other believers, so as to demonstrate what it means to be a servant to all. Thank you, Father, for sending your Son to us. In Jesus' name, amen!

Adapted from Luke 23:46; Jeremiah 29:11;
Psalm 73:25; 119:9–11; Ephesians 6:7; 5:21

GROWING IN *Prayer*

1. What connotations arise when you hear the word *submission*?

2. What do you think it means to put yourself into someone else's hands?

3. What kinds of associations do you have with the term *the Father's hands*?

4. Read Luke 23:44–46. If you had been an observer of these occurrences, how would you have reacted?

5. React to this statement: "The only prayer that needs to be prayed is, 'Into your hands I commit myself.'"

6. How could submission occur through prayer?

7. In what areas of your life do you struggle with submission to God?

Chapter 14

Jesus' Prayers of Blessing

It has always been interesting to me that when a student sneezed in the classroom, at least a few kids would say, "God bless you." While I might also have *thought* that little blessing prayer myself, I would not have said it aloud. The practice is so ingrained in many of us, though, that it's a natural part of our everyday interactions. Some people say "Blessings!" when they say good-bye—and others use that as a closing to a note or email. Southerners say, "Bless your heart," which, depending on the tone of voice, could be a good thing or a not-so-good thing. In any case, it's a largely unnoticed social practice that has existed for centuries, perhaps stemming from biblical times.

Jesus prayed blessings on others and instructed his disciples to do the same. We do not have a specifically quoted prayer of blessing that Jesus actually spoke—simply references that he said one. After his resurrection and appearance to the disciples, he blessed them:

> When he had led them out to the vicinity of Bethany, he lifted up his hands and blessed them. While he was blessing them, he

left them and was taken up into heaven. Then they worshiped him and returned to Jerusalem with great joy. And they stayed continually at the temple, praising God.

Luke 24:50–53

This truly is a touching scene. The disciples' friend, who just happened to be the Messiah, demonstrated his human affection for them. This scene, in fact, was the end of a dear friendship, as one commentator wrote, "so human, so natural, so utterly inartificial, that He lifted His hands to bless them, moved by the same impulse with which so often we have wrung a hand at parting, and stammered, 'God bless you!'"[1] When we love people, we pray God will bless them.

A commonality of the blessing prayers is that Jesus is blessing others, not asking for a blessing or favor for himself. Blessing others helps to usher them into worship. We see in the Luke 24:50–53 passage that the disciples' response is their worship of him, their own praise of the Father, and then their own time of prayer. From this point on, Scripture tells us the disciples were constantly united—in prayer (see Acts 1:14).

There are earlier references to blessings. When Jesus was teaching one day, Scripture tells us, "people were bringing little children to Jesus to have him touch them, but the disciples rebuked them" (Mark 10:13). Jesus got upset with them for this slight of the children, invited them to him, and said the kingdom of God belongs to "such as these" (v. 14). He then "took the children in his arms, put his hands on them and blessed them" (v. 16). Asking God to bless those whom power figures would ignore—children, the homeless, the elderly—certainly must be a prayer our Lord would hear.

Another reference to blessing occurs when Jesus instructed the disciples to bless the home of someone willing to house them as they traveled in pairs to spread the good news. He said, "When you enter a house, first say, 'Peace to this house.' If a man of peace is there, your peace will rest on him; if not, it will return to you" (Luke 10:5). I grew up in a traditional church that developed the practice of passing the peace. At an early point in the church service, those in the congregation would turn to their pew neighbors and say, "Peace be with you," and the recipient would respond, "And also with you." This is a greeting that Jesus used with his disciples (Luke 24:36; John 20:19, 26). In my family's church this was meant to be a prayer of blessing, because while Jesus can indeed convey peace on someone, we cannot. God alone does that kind of work. Yes, nations agree to peace treaties, and disagreeable neighbors can come to peace about a fence line. But actually grant someone peace of mind and soul and heart? That is God's business.

Asking God's Favor for Others

To bless someone is to invoke God's care for someone. These prayers are requests for God's protection and favor for someone else. It's a gift from one person to another via the heavenly Father. It's a form of intercession—one person's request on behalf of another—as opposed to petition, which is a request that would benefit the pray-er himself or herself (such as the give-us-our-daily-bread prayer). There are lots of ways we can ask God to bless people we know.

Bless him with good health, Lord.

Bless her with understanding so she can pass her final exams.

Father, bless them with the right house so they can serve you in this new community.

Bless them, God, with financial provision for the car they need.

Bless our lawmakers with insight so as to do your work, Father.

Bless the firefighters with your protection as they speed down the road and fight that fire, dear Lord.

Bless my children today with a sense of your presence at school.

While it's common to see a social media meme that says, "Bless me today, Lord," Jesus didn't pray for blessings and favor for himself. Does that mean it's not biblical to pray for favor for oneself? No, it's just that we do not have examples of *Jesus* doing that. However, we are blessed already if we know Jesus Christ as our personal Savior and Lord. He has already favored us with his presence, guiding hand, comfort, and purpose for our lives. Does that mean we can't ask God to prosper us, to make us successful and rich? Doesn't God want us to be happy? If I am learning about how to pray from the Master Teacher, I simply do not see him modeling that behavior. I don't need to pray, *Bless me, Lord,* because the blessing—he himself—is already within my grasp. In fact, he is living within me.

The Grace Blessing

The other type of blessing Jesus gave was a prayer of thanks over food. While the first kind of blessing prayer is for what you hope God will do for someone, the grace blessing is a prayer of thanksgiving for what God has already done. Here's the first example after the disciples presented Jesus with five loaves of bread and two fish.

And he directed the people to sit down on the grass. Taking the five loaves and the two fish and looking up to heaven, he gave thanks and broke the loaves. Then he gave them to the disciples, and the disciples gave them to the people. They all ate and were satisfied, and the disciples picked up twelve basketfuls of broken pieces that were left over. The number of those who ate was about five thousand men, besides women and children.

Matthew 14:19–21

This blessing over the food, or what we now call grace, was different from the Jewish norm. A Jewish grace—a very long recited prayer of thanksgiving—was said after the meal, based on a literal interpretation of Deuteronomy 8:10: "When you have eaten and are satisfied, praise the Lord your God for the good land he has given you." Note the sequence here for the Jewish grace: You would eat until satisfaction, then give praise to God for his provision.

Jesus did this differently. He mixed up tradition again. Even before the meager meal was miraculously multiplied, Jesus gave thanks. We might surmise he prayed the blessing in expectation that God would indeed not only provide but also satisfy the people—so much so that there were more leftovers than what they had before the miracle. John tells us that in the second of these feeding miracles, the thousands of people there—women and children undoubtedly adding to the five thousand men— got "as much as they wanted" (John 6:11). Getting more than you need or even want—certainly that is prospering. That is a blessing. That is favor above and beyond what we should expect and certainly more than we deserve.

The grace blessing I grew up with was this: "Bless, O Lord, these gifts to our use and us to thy service, and make us ever mindful of the needs of others. In Jesus' name, amen." There is no "bless me" in this prayer, either. We have a perspective of thankfulness for all we have been given, as well as an understanding that what God has given us is meant to equip us to serve others, which is effectively serving him. It's not a request that God bless us with the food but instead to use it for his work.

Praying blessings over others is Jesus' work. Intercession is selfless love in action. It is putting others' needs at the forefront of the Father's throne and saying, *Help her, Lord. Show her what you can do. Be magnified through a blessing to which she will testify and bring glory to you.*

This reminds me of a hymn my children and Craig and I learned in the small-town church where they grew up in the Sierra Valley, with a chorus that will always stick with me:

> Make me a blessing, make me a blessing,
> Out of my life may Jesus shine;
> Make me a blessing, O Savior, I pray,
> Make me a blessing to someone today.[2]

This prayerful chorus puts the blessing prayer into perspective. Our objective with a prayer of blessing is to understand that in the same way Jesus Christ has blessed us, we have the opportunity to bless others. That can start with the perspective of prayer, lifting up the needs of others to the heavenly Father, because out on those highways and byways of life, many need to know the love of a Savior. They truly are weary and sad and need the power that his forgiveness will provide and the peace that will pass all human comprehension.

Be blessed as you pray abundance for all those around you.

PRAYER FOR BLESSING

Father, please bless _____, who has been humbly mindful of you and all that you have provided. Do great things for this person for whom I care greatly. Show your mercy that covers all mistakes. Perform the seemingly impossible things in this person's life. Fill the hunger with good things—food, shelter, financial provision, the favor of a good job, friendships, and dear fellowship with you. Bless this person with your protection and guidance that points to the right decisions and the right life pathways. Provide a blessing of your dear presence and sense of tender love, patience, and joy only possible from the well-spring of your Word. And may this person understand that all blessings come through the filter of your sovereign hands and glorify you alone. In Jesus' name, amen!

Adapted from Luke 1:46–55, 68–79

GROWING IN *Prayer*

1. How has God recently blessed you?

2. Read Luke 24:50–51. While we don't have an actual prayer of blessing from Jesus, what might Jesus have said?

3. When someone tells you, "God bless you," how do you feel? When you say that to someone else, what motivates you to do so?

4. How would you feel about telling someone, "Peace be with you"? And how might others receive that kind of blessing?

5. Read Matthew 14:17–21. Jesus gave thanks for the food that would be miraculously multiplied to feed the thousands who had been listening to him teach on the hills overlooking the Sea of Galilee. Is it that important to say a blessing over each meal? Why or why not? What is your practice about saying grace?

6. Jesus didn't pray for blessings or favor for himself—only for others. How do you feel about that?

7. Someone you know needs a blessing prayer today. Pray . . . and reach out with a personal touch.

Conclusion

Jesus Lives to Pray

I mentioned earlier that I have written tons of recommendation letters for high school seniors over three decades of teaching—for college applications and for local, state, and national scholarship organizations. From the get-go I knew that my advocacy through a letter was critical for my students, most of whom came from lower-income families. After a period of time, I felt I had developed some influence, especially with organizations at the state and local levels, as my rural students competed for money, often besting students from very large schools. One parent told me, "You wrote an amazing letter about her character, accomplishments, and potential." I simply figured that was part of my job—to advocate on their behalf—and as scholarship organizations got to know me, they trusted my judgment and appraisal. Why did I work more than an hour on each letter? Because I loved my students and simply wanted the best for them.

This is true for Jesus, too. I use the word *is*, because he *still* advocates for us. He still prays for us. He still intercedes on our behalf. In the book of Hebrews we learn that Jesus is our great high priest who sympathizes with our weaknesses and stands ready to give immediate help when we need it (Hebrews 4:14–15). Historically, the high priest was chosen to represent the people before God with gifts and sacrifices to atone for their sins, and he could deal gently with those ignorant and misguided people, because he himself was "subject to weakness" (Hebrews 5:1–2). While men selected this high priest, it was understood that God had called the chosen man to this most important office to represent the people before God.[1] He was the intermediary—the mediator—between men and the Lord God. Because of their sin, the people could not approach God directly. However, with offerings in hand and with prayers, the high priest was the go-between for the people.

With Jesus' death as the final sacrifice, he became the final, perfect offering. And once he resurrected to be with the Father, he finished the order of the priesthood, which had started with Melchizedek (Hebrews 5:6; Genesis 14:18). God promises that Jesus now lives to mediate on our behalf as an intercessor:

Others became priests without any oath, but he became a priest with an oath when God said to him:

> "The Lord has sworn
>   and will not change his mind:
> 'You are a priest forever.'"

Because of this oath, Jesus has become the guarantee of a better covenant.

Now there have been many of those priests, since death prevented them from continuing in office; but because Jesus lives forever, he has a permanent priesthood. Therefore he is able to save completely those who come to God through him, because he always lives to intercede for them.

Hebrews 7:20–25

Jesus is our high priest. He is our intercessor. The Hebrew word for *intercessor* is translated as "mediator" and "spokesman."

Jesus, then, is our spokesman before the Father, and he *lives* to intercede for us. It's his job, so to speak.

When we falter and can't find the right words to give thanks or praise God or lament the gut-wrenching word bile out of our mouths, he is the perfect intercessor on our behalf. He knows the right words. He knows the right timing. He understands our situation because he lived on earth and suffered the same kinds of pain that we now do.

Jesus is in the intercession job constantly and permanently (Hebrews 7:24–25). We don't need to worry that he won't show up for his praying job someday. He is faithfully our intercessor.

He also meets our needs. He is holy and blameless and pure—set apart from the sin influences of the world, exalted even above the heavens (Hebrews 7:26). Jesus is the perfect high priest, the perfect spokesman. He doesn't need to take God an offering—a gift for the Host of heaven. When I worked at the high school and wanted a big favor from the teacher-in-charge, I would take her a bag of peanut M&Ms. She would do anything for a bag of peanut M&Ms. In fact, the year she retired, her seniors gave her a plaque with a bag of peanut M&Ms on it. But Jesus doesn't have to take the Father anything because he already has given the perfect gift: himself.

The Perfect Gift is interceding for YOU. He lives to intercede for you. So if you don't have the right words or the right timing or the right attitude, guess what? He does. You don't have to do this prayer thing perfectly. While the Father loves it when you go to him in prayer, when the world turns black and it feels as though you cannot find your way to the next moment, Jesus has already begun interceding for you.

And our Savior is a Master Teacher in communication. In fact, he began the conversation with you even before you were born. He was the One who said, "Here I am! I stand at the door and knock. If anyone hears my voice and opens the door, I will come in and eat with him, and he with me" (Revelation 3:20).

He not only is the way you are able to come to the Lord's Table for conversation, he is your table-talk advocate with the Father. Because he initiated the conversation and taught us to pray, we just need to make sure that door stays wide open. Listen in . . .

Father, as the Alpha and the Omega, I appeal to you on behalf of our servants. Consider their hard work and perseverance in the faith. They have endured hardships and yet keep pressing on. However, they have lost some of the passion for the faith and the desire to make you their first priority. They also have fears about what others will think if they fully live out their lives for you. Be merciful and gentle, Father. While you are completely faithful, a heavenly perspective is not always apparent to your creation on the earth. They are often tempted by the various lures of the world. We are not of the world, but they are surrounded by immorality. Daily they must make choices to serve you, and it is not easy—I know this because I, too, was tempted. Give them the strength to make the right decisions that will keep them on your sovereign and straight path. Turn them from wrong teachings and instead toward your Word, which is good and true. Be generous, Lord, with the fruits of your Spirit and with ministry giftings, that they will serve you with their whole hearts—not to please men but to honor you. Plant love within them with such deep roots that it bears fruit that is so appealing and delicious to those who do not yet believe that they taste and see it is good indeed and put their faith and trust in you. Cancel any attempt by the enemy to discourage or discredit your servants. Build them up in the faith, Father, so that in their strength they bring you honor and glory and praise. Thank you, holy Father. And so be it.

Adapted from Jesus' words to the
Seven Churches in Revelation 1–3

Notes

Foreword

1. E. Stanley Jones, *Abundant Living* (Nashville, TN: Abingdon Press, 2014), 228.

Chapter 1: Jesus Listened in Prayer

1. Kenneth Barker, ed., *The NIV Study Bible* (Grand Rapids, MI: Zondervan, 1985), 1541.

2. W.E. Vine, *An Expository Dictionary of New Testament Words* (Old Tappan, NJ: Fleming H. Revell Company, 1966), 200.

3. Vine, 234.

4. Rosalind Rinker, *Prayer: Conversing with God* (Grand Rapids, MI: Zondervan, 1983), back cover.

5. Rodney Reeves, "No, Prayer Isn't Really a Conversation," *Christianity Today*, June 11, 2015, http://www.christianitytoday.com/ct/2015/june-web -only/no-prayer-isnt-really-conversation.html.

6. Mother Teresa, *In the Heart of the World: Thoughts, Stories and Prayers*, as quoted in "Quotes about Prayer" on Goodreads.com, 2017, https://www .goodreads.com/quotes/tag/prayer.

7. Thomas à Kempis, *The Imitation of Christ: Classic Devotions in Today's Language*, ed. James N. Watkins (Franklin, TN: Worthy Inspired, 2015), 51.

Chapter 2: Jesus' Prayer in the Face of Temptation

1. J.D. Douglas, ed., *The New Bible Dictionary* (Grand Rapids, MI: Eerdmans, 1971), 419.

2. Douglas, 419.

3. Elmer L. Towns, *Fasting for Spiritual Breakthrough* (Ventura, CA: Regal Books, 1996), 14.

4. Towns, 14.

Chapter 3: Jesus' Prayer for Daily Needs

1. Jackie Bolden, The World Methodist Museum, email message to author, May 26, 2017.

2. *War Room*, directed by Alex Kendrick (2015; Franklin, TN: Provident Films, Affirm Films and TriStar Pictures, 2015), DVD.

3. W.E. Vine, *Expository Dictionary of New Testament Words* (Old Tappan, NJ: Fleming H. Revell Company, 1966), 190.

4. Vine, 146–47.

5. Richard Foster, *Prayer: Finding the Heart's True Home* (San Francisco: HarperSanFrancisco, 1997), 179–80.

6. Foster, 290.

Chapter 4: Jesus' Prayer of Praise

1. Bill Hybels, *Too Busy Not to Pray* (Downers Grove, IL: InterVarsity Press, 1998), 55.

2. *Merriam-Webster*, s.v. "praise," accessed May 25, 2017, https://www.merriam-webster.com.

3. Richard Foster, *Prayer: Finding the Heart's True Home* (San Francisco: HarperSanFrancisco, 1997), 81.

4. O. Hallesby, *Prayer* (Minneapolis: Augsburg, 1994), 142–43.

5. Becky Harling, *The 30-Day Praise Challenge* (Colorado Springs: David C. Cook, 2013), 17–18.

6. Janet Holm McHenry, *PrayerWalk: Becoming a Woman of Prayer, Strength and Discipline* (Colorado Springs: WaterBrook Press, 2001), 11–12.

Chapter 5: Jesus' Prayer of Thanksgiving

1. Mark Batterson, *The Circle Maker* (Grand Rapids, MI: Zondervan, 2011), 13.

2. Carole Lewis, *A Thankful Heart: How Gratitude Brings Hope and Healing to Our Lives* (Ventura, CA: Regal, 2005), 138–39.

3. Lewis, 141–42.

Chapter 6: Jesus' Prayer in Trouble

1. W.E. Vine, *Expository Dictionary of New Testament Words* (Old Tappan, NJ: Fleming H. Revell Company, 1966), 152.

2. Vine, 152.

Chapter 7: Jesus' Prayer for Himself

1. W.E. Vine, *Expository Dictionary of New Testament Words* (Old Tappan, NJ: Fleming H. Revell Company, 1966), 81.

2. Dan Dehaan, *The God You Can Know* (Chicago: Moody Publishers, 1982), 78.

3. Merriam-Webster, s.v. "logos," http://merriam-webster.com/logos.

4. Jennifer Kennedy Dean, *Live a Praying Life: Open Your Life to God's Power and Provision* (Birmingham, AL: New Hope Publishers, 2010), 37.

5. Charles Spurgeon, *The Power of Prayer in a Believer's Life* (Lynnwood, WA: Emerald Books, 1993), 140.

Chapter 8: Jesus' Prayer for Friends

1. Kenneth Barker, ed., *The NIV Study Bible* (Grand Rapids, MI: Zondervan, 1985), notes, 1630.

2. Herbert Lockyer, *All the Prayers of the Bible* (Grand Rapids, MI: Zondervan, 1959), 226.

3. Lockyer, 226.

4. "5479. Chara," Bible Hub 2016, http://biblehub.com/greek/5479.htm.

5. W.E. Vine, *Expository Dictionary of New Testament Words* (Old Tappan, NJ: Fleming H. Revell Company, 1966), 317.

Chapter 9: Jesus' Prayer for the Church

1. Kenneth Barker, *The NIV Study Bible* (Grand Rapids, MI: Zondervan, 1985), notes, 1631.

2. Everett F. Harrison, *The Wycliffe Bible Commentary* (Chicago: Moody Press, 1971), 1113.

3. Barker, 1631.

4. Harrison, 1113.

5. "Intercession," https://www.google.com/search?q=intercession&oq=intercession&aqs=chrome..69i57j0l5.2158j0j4&sourceid=chrome&ie=UTF-8#q=intercession+definition.

6. Charles H. Spurgeon, "Intercessory Prayer," The Spurgeon Archive, August 11, 1861, https://archive.spurgeon.org/sermons/0404.php.

7. Herbert Lockyer, *All the Prayers of the Bible* (Grand Rapids, MI: Zondervan, 1959), 227.

Chapter 10: Jesus' Prayer over Critical Decisions

1. Janet Holm McHenry, *Daily PrayerWalk: Meditations for a Deeper Prayer Life* (Colorado Springs: WaterBrook, 2002), 150.

Chapter 12: Jesus' Prayer in Abandonment

1. Jesus spoke in Aramaic here with some Hebrew characteristics, Aramaic being the common spoken language of the time (whereas the early manuscripts are mostly found in Hebrew). Both Matthew and Mark record this prayer, while John does not, as he would have taken Jesus' mother, Mary, away from the scene by that time.

Kenneth Barker, ed., *The NIV Study Bible* (Grand Rapids, MI: Zondervan, 1985), 1529. "What Language Did Jesus Speak?" Zondervan Academic,

September 7, 2016. http://zondervanacademic.com/blog/what-language-did
-jesus-speak/.

2. Barker, 805.

3. Barker, 805.

4. L.B. Cowman, *Streams in the Desert: 366 Daily Devotional Readings*,
James Reimann, ed. (Grand Rapids, MI: Zondervan, 1997), 13.

5. W.E. Vine, *Expository Dictionary of New Testament Words* (Old Tappan, NJ: Revell, 1966), 126.

6. Janet Holm McHenry, *PrayerWalk: Becoming a Woman of Prayer,
Strength and Discipline* (Colorado Springs: WaterBrook, 2001), 160–62.

7. St. John of the Cross, *Dark Night of the Soul* (New York: Image Books/
Doubleday, 1990), 119.

Chapter 13: Jesus' Prayer of Submission

1. Kenneth Baker, ed., *The NIV Study Bible* (Grand Rapids, MI: Zondervan,
1985), notes, 1635.

2. W.E. Vine, *Expository Dictionary of New Testament Words* (Old Tappan, NJ: Revell, 1966), 210.

3. Richard J. Foster, *Prayer: Finding the Heart's True Home* (San Francisco:
HarperSanFrancisco, 1997), 47.

Chapter 14: Jesus' Prayers of Blessing

1. "Luke 24:50–51," MacLaren's Expositions, BibleHub, 2004–2017. http
://biblehub.com/commentaries/luke/24-50.htm.

2. Ira B. Wilson, "Out in the Highways and Byways of Life," *Hymns for
the Living Church* (Carol Stream, IL: Hope Publishing Company, 1974), 505.
Note: The lyrics were written in 1909 and are in the public domain.

Conclusion: Jesus Lives to Pray

1. Kenneth Barker, ed., *The NIV Study Bible* (Grand Rapids, MI: Zondervan,
1985), 1863.

Janet McHenry has been featured in magazines such as *Health*, *Family Circle*, and *First*, and is recognized as an authority on prayer and prayerwalking—speaking on radio programs and at national conferences about the prayer life of Jesus, whom she calls her personal trainer or prayer mentor. She is the author of twenty-three books, including the bestselling *PrayerWalk: Becoming a Woman of Prayer, Strength, and Discipline.*

Janet and her rancher husband, Craig, have raised four children in the Sierra Valley in northeastern California, where she taught high school English most of her twenty-six years of teaching. She serves as the director of prayer ministries at The Bridge Church in Reno, where she leads an annual prayerwalk for the schools. She also has served as county director for Moms in Touch International (now Moms in Prayer) and as the prayer coordinator for the Advanced Writers and Speakers Association.

Besides walking and hiking, Janet enjoys kayaking with Craig and spoiling her ten grandchildren. Most of all, though, she enjoys hearing from readers and connecting with others as she speaks around the country to churches and other groups. You may contact her through her website, www.janetmchenry.com.